Put That In Writing

Level One

Mastering the Paragraph

with revised and expanded rubrics

By Steve & Shari Barrett

Put That In Writing
Level One

Published by:
Barrett's Bookshelf
16165 S.W. Inverurie Road
Lake Oswego, Oregon 97035
www.BarrettsBookshelf.com

© 2002 by Steven E. and Sharon R. Barrett.
All rights reserved. Published 2003. April 2006 printing.

No part of this book may be reproduced, stored in a retrieval system, or transmitted in any form by any means, electronic, mechanical, graphical, photocopying, recording, or otherwise without written permission from the authors.

ISBN 0-9728731-0-4

Cover photo by Susan Buck
Cover design by Jeff Barrett

To Our Lord and Savior who so faithfully calls us to God-sized challenges that only He could accomplish. All glory is His.
-Steve & Shari

To Mrs. Neeley who modeled how to teach in a manner that reaches students' hearts, and without whom I would not have known enough grammar to produce this text. You are one of a kind, and hundreds of students know it!
-Shari

Special thanks also go to Telisa Vale, Karen Haas, and "The Thinkers."

Put That In Writing

Table of Contents

To the Teacher iii
To the Student vi
Week 1:   Sentence Savvy Lesson 1
          Week 1:   Daily Assignments 5
Week 2:   Formal Writing Guidelines Lesson 9
          Week 2:   Daily Assignments 14
Week 3:   The Purposes of Writing Lesson 19
          Week 3:   Daily Assignments 22
Week 4:   The Writing Process Overview Lesson 27
          Week 4:   Daily Assignments 32
Week 5:   Paragraph Basics 1 Lesson 37
          Week 5:   Daily Assignments 42
          Week 6:   Daily Assignments 46
Week 7:   Paragraph Basics 2 Lesson 51
          Week 7:   Daily Assignments 56
          Week 8:   Daily Assignments 60
Week 9:   Descriptive Paragraphs Lesson 63
          Week 9:   Daily Assignments 67
Week 10: Research, Documentation, and Ownership of Ideas Lesson 71
          Week 10: Daily Assignments 77
Week 11: Definition Paragraphs Lesson 81
          Week 11: Daily Assignments 84
Week 12: Thinking Like a Teacher Lesson 87
          Week 12: Daily Assignments 91
          Week 13: Daily Assignments 95
Week 14: Narrative Paragraphs Lesson 97
          Week 14: Daily Assignments 101
          Week 15: Daily Assignments 104
          Week 16: Daily Assignments 107
Week 17: Process Paragraphs Lesson 111
          Week 17: Daily Assignments 114
          Week 18: Daily Assignments 117
          Week 19: Daily Assignments 120
Week 20: Comparison Paragraphs Lesson 123
          Week 20: Daily Assignments 127
          Week 21: Daily Assignments 130
          Week 22: Daily Assignments 133
Week 23: Cause or Effect Paragraphs Lesson 137
          Week 23: Daily Assignments 141
          Week 24: Daily Assignments 144
          Week 25:Daily Assignments 147
Week 26: Analogy Paragraphs Lesson.. 151
          Week 26: Daily Assignments 154
          Week 27: Daily Assignments 157

Week 28: Daily Assignments	159
Week 29: Defending a Position Lesson	163
Week 29: Daily Assignments	167
Week 30: Daily Assignments	170
Week 31: Daily Assignments	172
Week 32: Character Analysis Lesson	175
Week 32: Daily Assignments	180
Week 33: Daily Assignments	183
Week 34: Daily Assignments	185
Week 35: Seeing the Big Picture	187
Week 35: Daily Assignments	191
Week 36: Final Exam	195
Appendix A - Verbs, Conjunctive Adverbs, Subordinating Conjunctions	199
Appendix B - Prepositions, Style Points, Formality and Grammar Rules	200
Appendix C - Paragraph Checklist	201
Appendix D - MLA Documentation	202
Appendix E - Week 5 and Week 6 Paragraph Evaluation Form	206
Appendix F - General Paragraph Grading Form	207
Appendix G - Week 10 Research & Documentation Evaluation Form	208
Appendix H - Timed Paragraph Grading Form	209
Appendix I - Edit Evaluation Form	210
Appendix J - Teaching Schedules	211
Selected Bibliography	212
Index	213

To The Teacher

This course was birthed out of a need for a text that matched and supported my teaching goals. Whatever I teach, it is always my goal to see my students develop the abilities to think and communicate clearly so that they may have the greatest positive impact on those around them. While many good curricula are available, none seemed to combine all the elements I felt were necessary to achieve my goal. Therefore, I began to document the principles and materials I was teaching. Many of my former students have returned to tell me how the basics learned through this paragraphs course, and through my essays class, have benefited them both academically and professionally. With the encouragement of others, I have now drafted my teaching approach into a formal format which I hope will be beneficial to other instructors as well.

What are the goals of this course?
This course strives to give students:
- The ability to write with formality;
- The ability to develop properly-structured, logical paragraphs;
- The ability to edit a composition and enhance style;
- The ability to properly research and document;
- The ability to write for any academic or employment setting;
- The ability to write under the pressure of time.

What is the target grade level of this course?
This course is not targeted to a specific grade level as much as it is intended for the student who is academically ready to move on to full paragraphs and is capable of grasping the concepts of paragraph structure. Generally, the learning of paragraph writing at the level taught in this course should occur during seventh and eighth grades as this is usually when students acquire the necessary cognitive skills. This course could be appropriate for an advanced fifth or sixth grade student if the pace is slowed to allow the student to comprehend and master the concepts. High school students, and many of them fill my classes, would also benefit from this course if they need a greater understanding of what constitutes a good paragraph. This is a "skill level" rather than a grade specific course. Mastery of paragraph development is the goal.

What is the prerequisite for this course?
Students embarking on this course should be strong in grammar basics. Traditionally, grammar basics were mastered by the end of eighth grade; thus, the student should have already completed a thorough grammar program in order to be prepared to begin this course. Just as a mechanic must know the parts of an engine and their functions, the writer must know the parts of speech and their functions within the sentence in order to create effective paragraphs and essays.

What length of paragraphs should my students produce?
Lengths of paragraphs will vary; however, as a rule, junior high age students should start with a target of seven sentences per paragraph and progress beyond this length as

they go through the course. High school students should start out producing about ten sentence paragraphs, increasing the number as they progress. For most students, this will come easily if they will faithfully prepare good planning outlines and logically present the topic. Beyond these general guidelines, the instructor must determine an appropriate expectation for each student according to ability. The principle to employ is to ensure that students consistently strive to improve rather than become comfortable with meeting some minimum standard.

What does it mean to "drill" the grammar components included in this course?

Drill means training by repetition. In this course, students will be introduced to lists of items to memorize and rehearse orally or in writing. These rehearsals should be done every day in order to cement the ideas in the student's mind. The analogy I use for this in my classes and seminars is that water wears away stone one drip at a time. In the same manner, the drills "wear" patterns in the mind that last.

What comprises the Formality Drills and Style Drills in this text?

Formality Drills come from the points detailed in Week 2 on pages 9 through 13. Style Drills train the student to identify structures taught in Week 7 on pages 51 through 55. In both of these drills, the student must identify an error and rewrite the sentence correctly.

How is this text to be used?

This text is designed as a non-consumable. Thus, the student will need to write exercise answers on separate paper. Additionally, the instructor will need to make enough copies of the following items to use during the course.

1. Appendix B - Reference lists of prepositions, style points, formality and grammar items.
2. Appendix C – Paragraph Checklist: to be completed and submitted with assignments specified on the form.
3. Appendixes E through I – Evaluation Forms: for teacher and student use when evaluating student work and sample paragraphs in the text. These are designed to be used in specific weeks, and are marked accordingly.
4. The paragraphs on pages 91, 92, 93, 94, 95, 107-108, 120, 133, 147, 159, 172, and 185, so the students may mark the errors as they do the evaluation exercises.

How do I prepare to teach this course?

Naturally, familiarity with the material is essential. You should read the content and be certain that you understand the concepts. The information presented in Week 12 will be crucial to study since it explains the General Paragraph Grading Form (Appendix E) and how to evaluate a paragraph. Familiarize yourself with the basic questions listed in this lesson and do several practice evaluations so that when you correct your student's work, you will have developed a basis for evaluation. Turn to it frequently when you are grading and ask yourself if your student followed the requirements. Do not be afraid to grade critically if you know your student to be capable of doing better. Learning to write well is hard work and students may not perform without encouragement and prodding.

Writing with skill will only develop if there is continuous pressure to write at the level of capability. When your student resubmits work after the edit week, I recommend that you work back through the grading form to be certain that the student did all that you asked him to do. If he did not, turn it back for another correction. Preparation for teaching this class, then, centers on becoming familiar with the material and preparing yourself to correctly evaluate the student's work.

Additional preparation is needed for Week 10, when students will practice recording research as explained on pages 77-78. This drill will require the use of an encyclopedia and other source books on: the solar system, Samuel Clemens, and George Washington Carver. You will need to be certain that those resources are available when they are needed.

What is the recommended teaching schedule?
This text is set up for a thirty-six week course, that is, one school year. Once basic information about paragraphs is covered, different types of paragraphs are taught in a three week cycle. During the first week of the cycle, the student creates an original paragraph. In the second week, he prepares to write a paragraph under time constraints on Day 5. The third week, the pupil receives the graded paragraph written in the first week, edits it during the week, and resubmits it for a second grading on Day 5. I have found that requiring students to correct their work is critical in helping them make genuine progress. Otherwise, students tend to repeat errors over and over until they no longer recognize them as errors. Also, a practice I have employed as incentive to get my students to perform well is to give them the edit week off if the score on their first paragraph submission is 94% or above.

The course may either be expanded to fit a slower pace, or abbreviated for a shorter schedule. Suggested teaching schedule options are listed in Appendix G. Regardless of the teaching schedule you choose, be sure to allow sufficient time to evaluate papers and return them to the student.

In closing, it is my hope that this course proves beneficial for you and your student. In order to prepare your student for starting this course, he or she should read the "To The Student" section on the next page. If you or your students have comments or questions, I can be reached through our web page: <www.barrettsbookshelf.com>. I would love to hear from you.

Sincerely,

Shari Barrett

To The Student

You, the student, have been my greatest challenge in writing this course. Why? The reason is that, while I have recorded the mechanics of writing, I cannot come into your home or classroom and impart to you my vision for writing. How important is written communication? Written and spoken words are the means for preserving what we know and for communicating vision and purpose to those around us. Regardless of the calling on your life, you will need the skill of communicating clearly to those with whom you come in contact. Enabling you to do so with well-written paragraphs is the goal of this course.

As explained in a number of places in this course, language development follows a natural progression. First, a child develops the mastery of words. At the word level, one must work on phonics which leads to proper spelling skills. Upon this first component is built the next level of language usage: the sentence. It is at this level that you must grasp grammar, which includes proper punctuation. Too many students see grammar as unimportant. Like a master mechanic knows the components of an automobile engine, a strong writer knows sentence components. Therefore, start now to develop a vision for mastering grammar. It will serve you well. Strong grammar and well-written sentences form the foundations for strong paragraphs.

The steps in this process overlap as our knowledge and skill continually increase during our lives. Vocabulary improves, and we become more adept at creating interesting sentences. As sentences improve, our paragraphs grow more complex. However, progress becomes restricted if the basic building blocks are not mastered. Working at mastery is your job for this course.

It can be easy when one is in school to wonder when the skills being taught will ever be used. I cannot say when or if you will ever use all the concepts you are asked to learn; however, I do know you will need the skills taught in this course. It may be in a work setting where you write a letter or memo. It may be when you write a note to your child's teacher. It may even be as a soldier in the military, as our son has found. Wherever you go, whatever you do, communication will be necessary. My true vision for you goes beyond your education and career, however. Imagine that your grandchild wanted to be a writer and needed your help to become strong in the "building blocks" of writing. Would you be prepared? I also believe that as you are learning these concepts, larger lessons of proper attitude, perseverance, and self-discipline will be learned if you are willing. Will you persevere? Work at developing your vocabulary. Work at thinking logically. Work at communicating clearly. It will pay untold dividends in your life!

Shari Barrett

WEEK 1
Lesson: *Sentence Savvy*

1.1 Introduction

A clear understanding of sentence structure is the first step in writing effective paragraphs and essays. Most students are familiar with the common sentence types: declarative, interrogative, imperative, and exclamatory. However, in order to develop the ability to write in an interesting manner, four basic sentence structures must be mastered. Good writers emphasize important points, heighten readers' interest, and enhance readability by the way they vary sentence structure. This unit is a review of the four basic sentence structures: simple, compound, complex, and compound-complex.

> **Simple sentences are composed of a single independent clause.**

1.2 Simple Sentence

The first and easiest sentence structure is the **simple sentence** which is composed of a single **independent clause**. A **clause** is a cluster of words that contains a **subject** and a **predicate.** It can function as a single part of speech within a sentence, or as a sentence by itself. A clause is said to be "independent" when it can stand alone as a complete sentence.

> *Mary had a little lamb.*

Even if the above sentence had multiple subjects or multiple verbs, it would still be a simple sentence:

Multiple Subjects: *Mary, John, Joe, Bill, Betty, and Lois had a little lamb.*
Multiple Verbs: *Mary herded, fed, watered, and sheared her little lamb.*

> **A clause is a cluster of words with a subject and predicate that can function independently or as a single part of speech.**

Furthermore, if a sentence had multiple subjects <u>and</u> multiple verbs, it would <u>still</u> be a simple sentence:

> *Mary, John, Joe, Bill, Betty, and Lois herded, fed, watered, and sheared their little lamb.*

> **Verb:** Shows action or state of being.
>
> **Predicate:** Includes the verb and other words used to explain action or condition.

1.3 Compound Sentence

A sentence changes from a simple sentence to a **compound sentence** when two equivalent and related independent clauses (simple sentences) are connected by a coordinating conjunction, a semi-colon, or a semi-colon plus conjunctive adverb. **Coordinating conjunctions** (for, and, nor, but, or, yet, so) and semi-colons make uncomplicated connections:

Coordinating Conjunction: *Jack and Jill went up the hill, but Jack tumbled down.*
Semi-Colon: *Jack and Jill went up the hill; Jack tumbled down.*

> *The wavy-underline indicates an independent clause.*

> **Compound sentences contain two related independent clauses joined by a coordinating conjunction, semi-colon, or semi-colon plus conjunctive adverb.**

Conjunctive adverbs, on the other hand, both connect the independent clauses and show how they relate to one another. To be used properly, a semi-colon must follow the first clause, and the conjunctive adverb is set off by a comma:

Conjunctive Adverb: <u>Jack and Jill went up the hill</u>; then, <u>Jack tumbled down</u>.

Each underlined part in the above sentences is an independent clause which can stand alone without the other. Notice that there is a subject and verb on both sides of the "connector." If there were not a subject *and* verb both before and after the "connector," the sentence would be simple, having only one independent clause:

<u>Jack</u> and <u>Jill</u> <u>went</u> up the hill, but <u>tumbled</u> down.

Additionally, a compound sentence may contain numerous subjects and verbs in each independent clause:

The <u>driver</u> and <u>passenger</u> <u>were</u> both <u>injured</u> in the crash, but the <u>shopkeeper</u>, <u>pedestrian</u>, and <u>onlookers</u> all <u>escaped</u> injury.

1A - Common Conjunctive Adverbs *

accordingly	in addition	nevertheless	thereafter
consequently	likewise	otherwise	therefore
furthermore	meanwhile	still	thus
however	moreover	then	

* See Appendix A (page 199) for a more extensive list.

1.4 Complex Sentence

The next level of sentence structure is the **complex sentence**. This is a sentence comprised of one independent clause and one or more **dependent (subordinate) clauses**. The dependent clause is generally created by the use of a **subordinating conjunction**, which connects two unequal ideas. That is, one of the ideas is made *dependent* on the other.

> **Complex sentences have one independent clause and one or more dependent clauses.**

The students did not complete the assigned task **since** *they were out of time*.
or,
Since *the students were out of time*, they did not complete the assigned task.

Dotted underline indicates a dependent clause.

In the above examples, "since" serves to subordinate the idea of the students' lack of time to the main idea that the task was not completed. The main idea is made most important and the subordinate clause offers supporting information.

Even if additional subordinate (dependent) clauses are added, the sentence remains a **complex sentence**.

> *After the ski trip was over, the students did not complete the assigned task since they had run out of time.*

1B - Common Subordinating Conjunctions

after	as soon as	so that	where
although	because	than	which
as	before	that	while
as if	if	when	

* See Appendix A (page 199) for a more extensive list.

1.5 Compound-complex Sentence

The fourth sentence structure, **compound-complex**, is made up of a compound sentence with one or more subordinate clauses. Remember that a compound sentence contains at least two independent clauses.

> *While the monkey raced around the enclosure, the zoo onlookers clapped their hands, and one little child let out a delighted squeal.*

> *As the bull raged, the matadors raced in every direction seeking to escape, but a small child, oblivious to the danger, wandered into the ring while the crowd watched in horror.*

Compound-complex sentences are made of two independent clauses with one or more dependent clauses.

The wavy underline indicates an independent clause, and the dotted underline indicates a dependent clause.

1.6 Mastering Variety

Mastery of diverse sentence patterns combined with a well-developed vocabulary equips a writer to state his exact point in an interesting and stylish manner. For instance, if a pupil wanted to communicate in some way that learning to write can be challenging and rewarding, the four different sentence patterns can accomplish this in differing degrees.

1C - The Four Basic Sentence Structures

1. Simple:	*The pursuit of writing well is very challenging and rewarding.*
2. Compound:	*Writing well is challenging, but its pursuit produces the benefits of strong communication skills.*
3. Complex:	*Although writing well is challenging, those who diligently pursue it reap the benefits of strong communication skills.*
4. Compound-complex:	*Writing well is challenging; however, those who diligently pursue it will reap the benefits of strong communication skills, as it is also rewarding.*

1D - Above sentences divided into clauses

	Independent	Dependent
1.	*The pursuit of writing well is very challenging and rewarding.*	
2.	*Writing well is challenging,* **but its pursuit produces the benefits of strong communication skills.**	
3.	*those reap the benefits of strong communication skills.*	Although writing well is challenging, *who diligently pursue it*
4.	*Writing well is challenging;* **however, those will reap the benefits of strong communication skills,**	**who diligently pursue it** as it is also rewarding.

NOTE: If you cannot clearly identify all subjects and verbs in the above clauses, review these basics in a grammar course.

Regardless of the composition topic, great variety can be accomplished by using these patterns. Remember that complex sentences can have one or more dependent clauses, and compound-complex sentences must contain at least two independent clauses combined with any number of dependent clauses as long as the ideas remain clearly stated. With practice, any sentence structure can be expanded significantly beyond the samples presented above.

1.7 Emphatic Locations

Emphatic location refers to the placement of ideas in a sentence in order to increase or decrease their impact on the reader. The two primary points of emphasis are the beginning of the sentence and the end of the sentence. The end position is the strongest emphatic location because ideas here are the last in the reader's mind. Understanding how to change sentence structure allows a writer to shift ideas to different locations in the sentence depending on what he wants to emphasize. In the following example, notice how the emphasis changes as the ideas are moved to various locations:

Nothing but the outer shell of the car was left after the fire was doused.

Nothing but the outer shell of the car was left after the firemen doused the fire.

After the fire was doused, nothing but the outer shell of the car was left.

After the fire was doused, nothing of the car was left but the outer shell.

Which sentence above has the strongest impact? Which sentence is weakest?

Emphatic Locations:

1. *End of sentence*
2. *First of sentence*

WEEK 1
Sentence Savvy

Daily Assignments
(Write answers to all Daily Assignments on a separate sheet of paper.)

A. Reading Assignment:
Carefully read the Week 1 Lesson, Section 1.1 and 1.2. Be certain that you understand the concept of the simple sentence.

B. Grammar Drill:
Write the following state of being verbs and helping verbs on an index card to use for daily memorization drill. Rehearse them <u>every</u> <u>day</u> with your teacher either orally or by writing them from memory. Knowing them will help you in coming lessons to identify passive voice sentences and avoid over use of these verbs. Begin memorizing the list.

State of being verbs: am, are, was, were, be, been, being, is

Helping (Auxiliary) verbs: have, has, had, do, does, did, can, could, shall, should, will, would, may, might, must

C. Lesson Exercise:
Copy the following simple sentences onto a separate sheet of paper. Then draw one line under the subject(s) and two lines under the verb(s) in each sentence:

1. The majestic Columbia River courses through an expansive gorge.
2. White foaming water rushes over Multnomah Falls and Horsetail Falls and cascades to the valley below.
3. Prevailing east winds stream through the Columbia Gorge, making it a world famous destination for windsurfers.

--- Day 2 ---

A. Reading Assignment:
Carefully read the Week 1 Lesson, Section1.3. Be certain that you understand the difference between simple and compound sentences.

B. Grammar Drill:
Drill the state of being verbs and helping verbs.

C. Lesson Exercise:
Again, copy these sentences onto a separate sheet of paper. Underline subjects once and

verbs twice. Place brackets [ ] around each clause. Circle any coordinating conjunctions that connect clauses. Then indicate whether each sentence is simple or compound.

1. A trek to the top of Multnomah Falls culminates with a stunning view of the Columbia Gorge.
2. The trail up the face of the cliff can be slippery, and one must watch out for falling rocks.
3. The tour group hoped to see Mount Saint Helens, but clouds obscured the view.
4. Jeff and Jason willingly hosted the out of town visitors and offered their rooms to the welcome guests.

Day 3

A. Reading Assignment:
Carefully read Week 1 Lesson, Section 1.4. Be certain that you understand the distinction between a compound and a complex sentence.

B. Grammar Drill:
Drill the state of being verbs and helping verbs.

C. Lesson Exercise:
Again, copy these sentences onto a separate sheet of paper. Underline subjects once and verbs twice. Place brackets [ ] around each clause and circle any coordinating conjunctions that connect clauses. Then indicate whether the following sentences are simple, compound, or complex.

1. The soggy camping trip, which had begun in the Redwoods, ended at Newport, Oregon.
2. In order to keep the tent from leaking, the family spread tarps over the makeshift structure.
3. Although this precaution was taken, the next morning the family awoke to their tent standing in six inches of water.
4. Mother and Father put the young children in the car, and the parents began to fill the car-top carrier with camping gear.
5. The inclement weather had finally won.
6. After days of camping in the rain and visiting numerous laundromats, the defeated campers headed home.

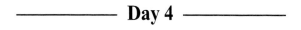

Day 4

A. Reading Assignment:
Carefully read the Week 1 Lesson, Section 1.5. Take notice of the difference between compound and compound-complex sentences.

B. Grammar Drill:
Drill the state of being verbs and helping verbs.

C. Lesson Exercise:
Again, copy the following sentences onto a separate sheet of paper. Underline subjects once and verbs twice. Place brackets [ ] around each clause and circle any coordinating conjunctions that connect clauses. Then indicate whether the sentences are simple, compound, complex, or compound-complex.

1. When the front door swung open, the dog ran for freedom.
2. Before anyone saw the dog's direction, he sneaked into the back yard, and he dodged into the underbrush, chasing a startled black cat.
3. Yes, the black cat was his most hated enemy.
4. Everyone knew that the dog would lose in a fight with his charcoal-colored enemy, so they installed a long chain for restraining the foolish canine.
5. To taunt the dog, the frisky feline stayed just out of the animal's reach.
6. To this day, the dim-witted dog chases the cat to the end of the restraining chain even though he flies through the air like a rocket when he hits the end of the tether.

D. Writing Exercise:
Write four sentences that demonstrate each of the basic sentence structures (one simple, one compound, one complex, one compound-complex), using the same general topic in each sentence. Mark all subjects and verbs so that you can clearly see the clauses.

Day 5

A. Reading Assignment:
Finish the Week 1 Lesson by reading the section 1.6 Mastering Variety and 1.7 Emphatic Location.

B. Grammar Drill:
Drill the state of being verbs and helping verbs.

C. Lesson Exercise:
On a separate sheet of paper, answer the following questions using complete sentences.

1. Based on the information in this lesson, which location in the sentence gives an idea the strongest emphasis?
2. What is the second strongest point of emphasis in a sentence?
3. Why would a knowledgeable writer shift an idea to the end of a sentence?

D. Writing Exercise:
1. Write a sentence which has the word "accident" in the greatest point of emphasis.
2. Rewrite the above sentence with the word "accident" moved to the second most emphatic location. Underline the most emphasized word or phrase in this new sentence.
3. Write four sentences that demonstrate each of the basic sentence structures, using the same general topic in each sentence. Mark all subjects and verbs so that you can clearly see the clauses.

WEEK 2

Lesson: *Formal Writing Guidelines*

2.1 Formal versus Informal Writing

Formal writing differs from informal writing in that it is more structured, requiring proper grammar, correct use of words, and strict attention to form. **Informal writing** is less structured, and everyday conversational language is permitted. When writing formally, however, the student must realize that one does not "write just like we talk." This may be a difficult distinction for a student to make if the student's primary work to this point has been "creative" writing or journaling. Nevertheless, formal writing is required in high school, college, and business, making it an essential skill for success in these areas. Therefore, this course is designed to develop a mastery of formal writing fundamentals through instruction and practice.

Formal writing requires strict attention to proper form.

2.2 Eliminate common informal practices

A. *Contractions*

Contractions are condensed forms of two words. While acceptable in conversational language, they are to be avoided in order to maintain the proper level of formality in writing.

  Informal: *Jay can't climb up the hill because his pack mule won't budge.*
  Formal: *Jay cannot climb up the hill because his pack mule will not budge.*

B. *Colloquial wording*

Colloquial refers to words used in casual, informal conversation or talk, rather than in formal speech or writing. Some people think of this term as referring to speech from a specific geographic region, but the meaning is much broader. Some examples of colloquialisms are:

  Informal: *He <u>busted</u> his arm.*
  Formal: *He broke his arm.*

  Informal: *When the news came, he <u>hit the ceiling</u>.*
  Formal: *When the news came, he became extremely upset.*

  Informal: *The child <u>wolfed</u> his food.*
  Formal: *The child ate his food very rapidly.*

C. Slang

Slang is the use of invented words in place of existing proper words, or words used apart from their true meanings. As such, slang generally does not convey precise meaning and changes quickly over time according to popularity.

1950's:	*Our family trip to Disneyland was really <u>swell</u>.*
1960's:	*Our family trip to Disneyland was really <u>cool</u>.*
1970's:	*Our family trip to Disneyland was really <u>groovy</u>.*
1980's:	*Our family trip to Disneyland was really <u>radical</u>.*
1990's:	*Our family trip to Disneyland was really <u>sweet</u>*

D. Clichés

A cliché is a timeworn expression which has lost its appeal.

A **cliché** is a timeworn expression which has been used so frequently that it is no longer appealing.

The woman went to the sale with her purse full of money and <u>shot the wad</u>. All of her plans for purchasing a new car went <u>up in smoke</u>.

E. *First and second person - avoid unless the assignment permits*

First person:	*I, me, my, we, us, our, ours*
Second person:	*you, your, yours*
Third person	*he, she, they, one, his, hers, theirs*

When the writer directly refers to himself (first person) or addresses the reader (second person), the formality of the writing is lowered. Even if the assignment requires the student to express his or her opinion, it is best to word the information in a way that does so without saying, "I think..." or "In my opinion..." When a sentence states a point of view, it is clearly the writer's position. Therefore, it is best to strive for wording which states information in the most formal fashion.

Informal:	*I believe that the basketball team played the best game of its season.*
Formal:	*The basketball team played the best game of its season.*
Informal:	*You will find the recipe to be pleasing to the eye and the taste buds.*
Formal:	*This recipe will be pleasing to the eye and the taste buds.*
Informal:	*In my opinion, the last presidential election was filled with voter fraud.*
Formal:	*The last presidential election was filled with voter fraud.*

F. Sentence fragments

The use of sentence fragments must be considered a literary tool which is to be used sparingly. Generally, these take on the characteristic of **interjections** which express emotion or opinion. However, they create a more conversational style which is not appropriate for formal writing. For example:

Informal: *Will the president veto the controversial legislation? Not likely.*

Formal: *Will the president veto the controversial legislation? A veto is not likely.*

An interjection is a word which conveys emotion and is usually punctuated as a sentence.

G. Ending a sentence with a preposition

Prepositional phrases start with a preposition and end with a noun. Therefore, prepositions should not be left alone to end a sentence. Rather, the wording should be modified as follows:

Informal: *Over there is the train he is riding on.*

Formal: *Over there is the train on which he is riding.*

Informal: *His mother asked him what he was going to the store for.*

Formal: *His mother asked what he was intending to purchase at the store.*

H. Nominalizations

A **nominalization** is using a word in its noun form when it would be best used as the verb in a sentence. While this is not truly a grammatical error, written composition will be stronger if verb forms are used rather than nouns.

Avoid: *The injured dog let out a yelp.*

Better: *The injured dog yelped.*

Avoid: *The toddler crossed the room with a stumble.*

Better: *The toddler stumbled across the room.*

Nominalization is using a word in its noun form when the verb form would be best.

2.3 Follow Grammar Rules

It is assumed that the student is familiar with grammar rules; therefore, the following grammar concepts are presented only briefly and do not represent a comprehensive list. If there are words or concepts mentioned here that are not understood, the authors recommend that the student use a grammar handbook to study those points. This section is only an attempt to point out the most common problems areas in student compositions.

A. Spelling and punctuation

Spelling and punctuation do matter. Whenever a student puts his thoughts into writing, he is representing himself with those words. Therefore, the standard must be high so that proper impressions are made in the mind of the reader. Even if spelling is a challenge, students should never give up making every effort to spell all words correctly. Proper punctuation also plays a significant role in clearly communicating meaning to the reader. Students must learn the rules and continue using them so that they are not forgotten. For some people, proper spelling and punctuation rules will be a lifetime challenge, but improvement will come with perseverance.

B. Subject-verb agreement

Subjects and verbs must agree in number. Number refers to singular or plural.

Singular: *The recliner rocks.*
Plural: *The recliners rock.*

C. Verb tense consistency

Verb tense should be as consistent as possible throughout a paragraph. **Tense** refers to the time of the action or state of being indicated by a verb: past, present, or future.

> *Tense refers to the time indicated by a verb.*

Incorrect: *Amanda was walking down the road when she sees a large dog.*
Correct: *Amanda was walking down the road when she saw a large dog.*

2A - Examples of verb tense

Past tense:	*was, did, saw,*
Present tense:	*is, does, sees,*
Future tense:	*will be, shall do, will see*

D. Antecedent clarity

Antecedents of pronouns must be clear. An **antecedent** is the noun or pronoun to which a pronoun refers.

> *An antecedent is the noun or pronoun to which a pronoun refers.*

Incorrect: *The soccer player hits the ball with his head; it rolls effortlessly into the goal.*
Correct: *The soccer player hits the ball which rolls effortlessly into the goal.*

E. *Person and number consistency*

Person must remain the same throughout the paragraph, and singular or plural forms of subjects and verbs must match within each sentence.

<u>Shift in person</u>

Improper: *The <u>student</u> must carefully plan the essay before writing. <u>You</u> then proceed to write a topic sentence.*

Proper: *The <u>student</u> must carefully plan the essay before writing. <u>She</u> then proceeds to write a topic sentence.*

<u>Shift in number</u>

Improper: *When <u>one</u> goes to the store, <u>they</u> should carefully compare prices of different brands.*

Proper: *When <u>one</u> goes to the store, <u>he</u> should carefully compare prices of different brands.*

F. *Use active voice*

Sentences are strongest when written in active voice. **Active voice** means the subject performs an action, whereas **passive voice** means the subject receives the action. Generally in passive voice, a state of being verb, acting as a helping (auxiliary) verb, accompanies an action verb. Thus state of being verbs can serve as markers for spotting possible passive voice sentences. However, the true test of whether a sentence is in active or passive voice is to determine whether the subject is doing or receiving the action.

Passive: *The soda can was crushed by Jason.*

Active: *Jason crushed the soda can.*

Active voice means the subject performs the action.

2.4 Conclusion

The following summarizes the Formality and Grammar Guidelines taught in this lesson:

General Guidelines
1. Have I eliminated contractions, colloquial wording, slang, clichés?
2. Have I written with the appropriate level of formality?
3. Have I eliminated sentence fragments, improper prepositions, and nominalizations?

Grammatical Guidelines
1. Have I corrected all spelling and punctuation errors?
2. Have I kept subjects and verbs in agreement?
3. Have I kept verb tenses consistent?
4. Are antecedents of pronouns clear?
5. Are person and number consistent?
6. Have I written as many sentences as possible in active voice?

Passive voice means the subject receives the action.

WEEK 2
Formal Writing Guidelines

Daily Assignments
(Write answers to all Daily Assignments on a separate sheet of paper.)

Day 1

A. Reading Assignment:
Read the entire Week 2 Lesson carefully. If there are terms you do not understand, look them up in a reference book or seek additional help from your instructor or someone who understands grammar.

B. Grammar Drill:
1. *Without looking at your cue card, write the state of being verbs and helping verbs on a blank sheet of paper and submit them to your instructor.*
2. *Indicate whether the following sentences are passive or active voice.*
   a. The rubber band hit the center of the target.
   b. The street below was hit by water balloons falling from above.

C. Sentence Drill:
1. *In the sentence below, underline the subject(s) once and the verb(s) twice. Place brackets [ ] around each clause and circle any coordinating conjunctions that connect clauses. Identify the structural type: simple, compound, complex, compound-complex.*

   Because they have so many working parts, determining what is wrong with an automobile can be very difficult.

2. *Rewrite the following sentence, placing the italicized word(s) in the most emphatic location.*

   Family photos were *neatly* displayed on the board.

D. Formality Drill:
Using the formality and grammar rules explained in this lesson, rewrite the sentences below in formal style:
1. She can't tell if the problem with the car is a dead battery or the ignition.
2. This music store carries compact discs by some really cool artists.
3. It is hotter than a pistol outside today.

Day 2

A. **Grammar Drill:**
   1. *Drill the state of being and helping verbs again today.*
   2. *Rewrite the following sentence in active voice.*

   The pitcher was dropped by the waiter.

B. **Sentence Drill:**
   1. *In the sentence below, underline the subject(s) once and the verb(s) twice. Place brackets [ ] around each clause and circle any coordinating conjunctions that connect clauses. Identify the structural type: simple, compound, complex, compound-complex.*

   The neighbor worked diligently to install the new waterfall and pond; however, one could only wonder if he would meet his deadline.

   2. *Rewrite the following sentence, placing the italicized word(s) in the most emphatic location.*

   The neighbor worked diligently to install the new waterfall and pond, but *one could only wonder* if he would meet his deadline.

C. **Formality Drill:**
Using the formality and grammar rules explained in this lesson, rewrite the sentences below in formal style:
   1. I think the large amount of paperwork had a negative impact on the teacher.
   2. Will the damaged car be repaired? Hopefully.
   3. He seen the deer while tramping through the woods.

Day 3

A. **Grammar Drill:**
   1. *Drill the state of being and helping verbs again today.*
   2. *Rewrite the following sentence in active voice.*

   His tent was crushed by the high winds.

B. **Sentence Drill:**
   1. *In the sentence below, underline the subject(s) once and the verb(s) twice. Place brackets [ ] around each clause and circle any coordinating conjunctions that connect clauses. Identify the structural type: simple, compound, complex, compound-complex.*

   Excavation, however, went quite rapidly.

2. Rewrite the following sentence, placing the italicized word(s) in the most emphatic location.

   In order to capture the lion, the young men strung a rope trap across the well-worn path.

C. Formality Drill:
Using the formality and grammar rules explained in this lesson, rewrite the sentences below in formal style:

1. The country was damaged greatly by the sudden tornado.
2. One must be thorough when you put out a campfire.
3. It was clear that the dogs was going to bite the mailman.

Day 4

A. Grammar Drill:
1. *Drill the state of being and helping verbs again today.*
2. *Rewrite the following sentence in active voice.*

   Colleen's dog was shocked by the black cat which streaked through the living room.

B. Sentence Drill:
1. *In the sentence below, underline the subject(s) once and the verb(s) twice. Place brackets [ ] around each clause and circle any coordinating conjunctions that connect clauses. Identify the structural type: simple, compound, complex, compound-complex.*

   When the day was over, the landscapers had accomplished much of their task.

2. *Rewrite the following sentence, placing the italicized word(s) in the most emphatic location.*

   Because their tastes bring back childhood memories, *berry pies and baked beans* are Elizabeth's favorite foods.

C. Formality Drill:
Using the formality and grammar rules explained in this lesson, rewrite the sentences below in formal style:

1. When the race car driver crossed the finish line, he sees his pit crew running to meet him.
2. It is my opinion that the Pilgrims were very brave when they came to the New World.
3. By the first spring, over one hundred of the Pilgrims had croaked.

Day 5

A. Grammar Drill:
1. *Drill the state of being and helping verbs again today.*
2. *Rewrite the following sentence in active voice.*

    Surprised were the tourists, by the size of Mount Rushmore.

B. Sentence Drill:
1. *In the sentence below, underline the subject(s) once and the verb(s) twice. Place brackets [ ] around each clause and circle any coordinating conjunctions that connect clauses. Identify the structural type: simple, compound, complex, compound-complex.*

    Tim and Colleen contemplated the landscape design for their new house and struggled to remove the largest rocks before the landscapers arrived.

2. *Rewrite the following sentence, placing the italicized word(s) in the most emphatic location.*

    Once the *underground sprinkler system* has been installed, it is too late to change the placement of the sod and shrubbery.

C. Formality Drill:
Using the formality and grammar rules explained in this lesson, rewrite the sentences below in formal style:

1. If Squanto hadn't helped the Pilgrims, they wouldn't have pulled through. *(hint: contains three informalities)*
2. The Pilgrims left the Dutch because their children were becoming so heathen.
3. William Brewster, John Carver, Edward Winslow, and William Bradford was some of the distinguished men who led this group.

WEEK 3

Lesson: *The Purposes Of Writing*

3.1 Introduction

All writing has one **general purpose**: to convey to the reader the exact idea that is in the mind of the writer. Precise choice of words is the first key to accomplishing this purpose. Therefore, a writer must utilize a well-developed vocabulary. Like an artist carefully mixing paints on a palette, the writer carefully combines words and phrases to convey to the reader a desired mental picture. This primary purpose extends across every form of writing.

In addition to the general purpose mentioned above, more specific purposes must be considered. Writing may also entertain, inform, or persuade. This course will not specifically cover writing for entertainment. However, all writing ought to, in some sense, entertain, in order to keep the reader's interest. *The primary emphasis here is formal writing in which* **information** *or* **persuasion** *is the goal*. Therefore, throughout this course, each writing assignment will have a specified purpose so students will learn to target a paragraph to inform or persuade.

> *The general purpose of all writing is to reproduce in the mind of the reader the exact mental picture that is in the mind of the writer.*

3.2 The Contention

The manner in which the writer begins a paragraph indicates its purpose. In a standard paragraph, the first sentence is called the **topic sentence** because it sets the topic for the paragraph. It also indicates the writer's **contention**, the argument which the writer plans to prove within the paragraph. For example, if one was to write a paragraph about exercise, the topic sentence might read as follows:

Consistent exercise produces positive results.

This opening sentence informs the reader that the topic is "exercise" and that the writer believes positive results come from consistent exercise. Thus, the reader will expect the balance of the paragraph to give evidence supporting this contention. Whether the purpose is to inform or persuade, a skilled writer prepares the reader to receive what he writes by beginning with an effective topic sentence that contains a clear contention.

3.3 Writing to Inform

Informative writing does exactly what the category indicates; that is, it presents information to the reader. When paragraphs are designed to inform, the topic sentence offers a **contention** to be proven, but the writer does not attempt to convince the reader to accept the contention. Instead this type of paragraph is characterized by a straight-forward presentation of facts, details, and analyses. Therefore, informative paragraphs are very common in reports and other writings where information and explanation rather than debate is the objective. Because of the heavy emphasis on imparting information, holding the reader's interest

> *A contention is the statement or point which one is defending.*

presents a challenge for the author. To solve this problem, the author should strategically insert creative wording, similes, metaphors, analogies, and humor.

3.4 Writing to Persuade

In contrast to the informative paragraph, the topic sentence of a persuasive paragraph should take a stronger position by presenting a contention that is a matter of opinion or strong conviction. A writer takes such a debatable position when asserting a viewpoint for which supporting evidence is unclear, lacking, or subject to different interpretations. On the other hand, the writer may believe the audience to be misinformed or lacking in understanding and desire to change its view on the subject. Then again, the writer may take a strong position in order to spur the reader to action. In any of these cases, swaying the reader through weight of evidence, argument, and appeal to accept the contention set forth in the topic sentence becomes the goal of the author.

When writing persuasively, the author plays the role of a lawyer offering evidence in a courtroom in support of his position on a subject that is debatable. Like an attorney building a case, he crafts his writing to show, in the most convincing way possible, that the evidence he presents supports his contention. The goal is to cause the reader to consider the writer's position and agree with it, or at least move closer to it. To succeed, the writer often must spend more time and go into more detail to explain how his contention is supported by the evidence. Facts, examples, principles, observations, personal experiences, authoritative evidence, and more may be used. The audience, like a jury, is invited by the tone of the writing to determine if the author has proven his case.

3.5 Unsupported Contentions

An unsupported contention is a statement or point offered as fact without supporting evidence to prove it true.

Whether writing to inform or persuade, a common error is to leave **unsupported contentions** within a paragraph. An **unsupported contention** is a statement offered as fact without any supporting evidence. Without proof, a reader has no reason to accept what an author writes. Therefore, to be effective, each statement, offered as fact, must be supported by evidence.

3.6 Conclusion

Illustrations 3A and 3B demonstrate the differences between informative and persuasive paragraphs. Although the topic sentence of the informative paragraph states a contention, the facts are presented in a manner strictly to inform the reader how it is that the housefly is dangerous. Appealing to the reader to accept the facts and conclusion is not attempted. By contrast, the writer of the persuasive paragraph seeks to convince the reader to agree with his conclusion by logical argument and direct appeal.

3A - Sample Informative Paragraph

Upon first glance, the pesky housefly seems to be only a nuisance; however, the insect is actually quite dangerous to mankind. With an irritating buzz and a sensory tickle, the housefly bothers man and beast alike, but one must look beyond this mild irritation to see the real threat from these scavenging insects. The danger results from the fly's food sources combined with the way it eats its food. Flies scavenge rotting material for food. Typical food sources include dead animals, discarded food scraps, manure in fields, and even open wounds. These are breeding grounds for such diseases as typhoid, dysentery, and cholera, along with many other bacteria and viruses. The second dangerous aspect is the fact that before eating, the fly secretes digestive juices onto its food to liquefy it. The fly then sucks up the liquefied food along with any dangerous germs. Whenever a fly secretes digestive juices, it deposits germs, picked up from wherever it previously fed, onto food in the home, into drink, and onto people. Therefore, not only should a fly swatter be kept close at hand, one should think twice before taking a bite when on one's picnic lunch a fly lands.

Sources cited on page 72.

3B - Sample Persuasive Paragraph

The "fat tax," currently being proposed in this country and elsewhere, should be opposed since it is inequitable and based upon flawed and dangerous reasoning. This tax would be levied on fast foods, soft drinks, snack foods, and other high fat items. While this may seem to be a positive move, inequity stands as the first flaw in this tax notion. The initial targets of the "fat tax" are fast food outlets. Since these restaurants serve inexpensive meals, a higher percentage of their clientele come from lower income families. Therefore, the greater share of the "fat tax" burden will be borne by lower income families. Why not levy the same tax at higher end eating establishments? They serve rich foods high in fat as well. The second reason to oppose this tax is the contradiction between its purpose and the intended use of funds. According to proponents, the tax will reduce consumption of high calorie foods (CSPI and Brownell). Simultaneously, supporters have immediate plans for spending the revenues on educating children in diet and exercise habits, health care for the overweight, and as a subsidy to poor families and producers of healthy foods. Herein lies the problem. If the tax works to diminish consumption of unhealthy foods, tax revenues will decrease. Meanwhile, programs dependent upon its revenue will have been created. How will these programs be maintained? In answer to this question, "fat tax" proponents reveal their more dangerous scheme. Its creators have announced future plans to apply the tax to other products deemed to contribute to obesity by encouraging a non-active lifestyle. Where will this end since so many products could be blamed for America's sedentary lifestyle? Already, proposals involve taxing video games and televisions (More Absurd). Obviously, instituting the "fat tax" opens the way to other unreasonable taxes. What about taxing recliners, sofas, cars, board games, or even books? For lawmakers, who already cannot seem to live within their fiscal income, the possibilities for expanding this tax appear unending. With such flawed and dangerous ideas as these, the "fat tax" should be starved out of existence.

Sources: "CPSI And Brownell." Internet. (June 4, 2002.) and "More Absurd Fat Tax Proposals." Internet. (March 1, 2000.) Available: www.consumerfreedom.com. Date accessed 18 July 2003.

WEEK 3
The Purposes of Writing

Daily Assignments

—— Day 1 ——

A. Reading Assignment:
Read the Week 3 Lesson carefully, making certain that you understand the material.

B. Grammar Drill:
1. *You should know the state of being verbs and helping verbs by now. Write them on a piece of paper and submit them to your instructor.*

2. *Begin to memorize the prepositions listed in Appendix B. Start with the first column. You are memorizing these so that you can identify prepositional phrases and avoid ending sentences with dangling prepositions.*

3. *Rewrite the following sentence in active voice.*

   The highly valuable baseball was hit out of the ballpark by Babe Ruth.

C. Sentence Drill:
1. *In the sentence below, underline the subject(s) once and the verb(s) twice. Place parentheses around any prepositional phrases. Place brackets [ ] around each clause and circle any coordinating conjunctions that connect clauses. Identify the structural type: simple, compound, complex, compound-complex.*

   A genuine friend encourages one to follow the right path, yet that friend still shows love when mistakes are made.

2. *Rewrite the following sentence, placing the italicized word(s) in the most emphatic location.*

   In order to ensure an *excellent* tape of the ceremony, the family made certain that several people operated video cameras.

D. Lesson Exercise:
Answer the following questions in complete sentences.

1. All writing has what general purpose?
2. What are the two primary purposes of formal writing taught in this text?
3. A standard paragraph begins with what kind of sentence?
4. Define "contention."
5. What is the challenge one faces when writing an informative paragraph? How is it overcome?
6. What is the goal when creating a persuasive paragraph?
7. Define "unsupported contention."

Put That In Writing 23

Day 2

A. Grammar Drill:
Drill the first column of prepositions again today.

B. Sentence Drill:
In the sentence below, underline the subject(s) once and the verb(s) twice. Place parentheses around any prepositional phrases. Place brackets [ ] around each clause and circle any coordinating conjunctions that connect clauses. Identify the structural type: simple, compound, complex, compound-complex.

In spite of the fact that some thought of him as unteachable, Thomas Edison became an eager learner.

C. Formality Drill:
Rewrite the following sentence to correct the informality:

Thomas Edison wasn't in school long before the schoolmaster expelled him.

D. Writing Exercise:
Using the same general topic, rewrite the following topic sentence so that it offers the reader a strong contention.

George Washington was the first president.

(Hint: Eliminating the state of being verb often helps to make a contention stronger.)
<u>Examples:</u>
Weak contention: *Thomas Edison was an inventor.*
Strong contention: *Edison crafted a number of useful inventions.*

Day 3

A. Grammar Drill:
Again, drill the first column of prepositions.

B. Sentence Drill:
In the sentence below, underline the subject(s) once and the verb(s) twice. Place parentheses around any prepositional phrases. Place brackets [ ] around each clause and circle any coordinating conjunctions that connect clauses. Identify the structural type: simple, compound, complex, compound-complex.

The result of one of Edison's experiments was a large explosion in the basement of his family's home.

C. Formality Drill:
Using the formality and grammar rules explained in Lesson 2, rewrite the sentence below in proper form:

Edison was so curious that he frequently finds himself in trouble.

D. Writing Exercise:
Using the same general topic, rewrite the following topic sentence so that it offers the reader a strong contention.

Ping pong is a game.

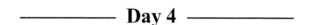

Day 4

A. Grammar Drill:
Drill the first column of prepositions again today.

B. Sentence Drill:
In the sentence below, underline the subject(s) once and the verb(s) twice. Place parentheses around any prepositional phrases. Place brackets [ ] around each clause and circle any coordinating conjunctions that connect clauses. Identify the structural type: simple, compound, complex, compound-complex.

Edison started earning his own living at age twelve, and at that same time, he built a laboratory for himself in a railroad car at the train station.

C. Formality Drill:
Using the formality and grammar rules explained in Lesson 2, rewrite the sentence below in proper form:

Most of Edison's life was spent like a square peg in a round hole.

D. Writing Exercise:
Using the same general topic, rewrite the following topic sentence so that it offers the reader a strong contention.

Computers are important.

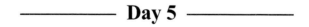

Day 5

A. Grammar Drill:
Drill the first column of prepositions again today.

B. Sentence Drill:
In the sentence below, underline the subject(s) once and the verb(s) twice. Place parentheses around any prepositional phrases. Place brackets [ ] around each clause and circle any coordinating conjunctions that connect clauses. Identify the structural type: simple, compound, complex, compound-complex.

During the Civil War years, Edison often worked behind battle lines as a roaming telegrapher.

C. Formality Drill:
Using the formality and grammar rules explained in Lesson 2, rewrite the sentence below in proper form:

Edison's invention, the phonograph, gave him international fame, and they were amazed at the simplicity of the device.

D. Writing Exercise:
Using the same general topic, rewrite the following topic sentence so that it offers the reader a strong contention.

The Lion, The Witch, And The Wardrobe is a book by C.S. Lewis.

WEEK 4

Lesson: *The Writing Process Overview*

4.1 Introduction

Many students dread writing assignments because they struggle with what to say and how to say it. This is due in large part to not having an orderly method of tackling the assignment, organizing ideas, and developing a good paragraph. Performance becomes much easier once the process is clearly understood. Therefore, what follows is a step-by-step process that will lead to the creation of well-developed paragraphs.

4.2 Preliminary Considerations

A. *Topic*

A writer's first responsibility is to know or decide what the topic is to be. An instructor may specify a topic, or the choice may be totally up to the student. In this second case, it is usually best to select a familiar topic so that it may be approached with more enthusiasm and require less research. Nevertheless, research may be necessary at any point in the planning and writing process.

B. *Purpose*

Next, the writer must know whether he is writing to inform or persuade. The purpose will influence both the content and arrangement of ideas. Therefore, it must be held clearly in mind to ensure that the paragraph does not lose focus and remains on topic.

C. *Audience*

Finally, a writer must know the **audience**. Audience can impact purpose, content, presentation, and approach to the subject. If the audience is well-informed on a specific topic, persuasion may be the best **purpose**. However, if the reader does not have even a basic knowledge of the topic under discussion, it will be absolutely necessary for the writer to take time to inform the reader. Secondly, the degree to which the audience is informed will also impact **content**: vocabulary, supporting information, and details. Thirdly, audience considerations also impact the manner in which information is **presented**. Is it best to write directly to the reader by addressing him? Should one include humor and employ other tools to maintain the reader's interest? Finally, the **approach** or perspective on the subject will be influenced by the audience. If, for instance, the writer is given the broad general topic of nutrition, the subject would most likely be discussed from one perspective if targeted to doctors and probably from another if written to mothers of young children. Thus, it is clear the differences in target audiences greatly affect a composition.

Preliminary considerations:
- *Topic*
- *Purpose*
- *Audience*

Choice of audience will impact purpose, content, presentation, and approach.

Brainstorming is listing any ideas associated with a topic.

4.3 Perspective

Taking the above into consideration, it is time to begin determining one's perspective on the assignment by a process called **brainstorming**. This process can be likened to a photographer who walks around an object, carefully studying various angles from which he might want to shoot the picture. From each angle, different ideas about the topic are generated. To illustrate, consider the differing ways in which one could approach the general topic of automobiles. Illustration 4A lists several perspectives, or ways to address the topic. From these many options, one approach must be chosen, keeping in mind the requirements of topic, purpose, and audience.

4A - Sample Perspective Brainstorming

Topic: Automobile
• development of the automobile • personal story of an auto experience • life of an automaker • evaluate a specific auto - pros and cons • compare two autos • compare the products of two auto makers • compare two classes (types) of vehicles • how improvements in autos have increased safety • how the auto is or is not significantly contributing to pollution • impact of the auto on travel • describe the classes of different types of automobiles • describe the different classes of engines which power automobiles

4.4 Preliminary Topic Sentence

When possible perspectives have been thought out, it is time to choose one idea and formulate it into a preliminary topic sentence. This sentence should clearly indicate the exact topic of the paragraph, the writer's contention, and the paragraph's purpose by its wording. Each of the above ideas could easily fill an essay; therefore, one should narrow the scope of the topic to fit within a paragraph. For example, if, from the above brainstorming strategy, the student chooses to write about improvements to autos, the drafted topic sentence might look something like these:

Informative paragraph: *Today's automobiles offer a number of safety features.*

Persuasive paragraph: *Some improvements in automobiles, designed to decrease fuel consumption, have resulted in more fatalities.*

A draft, such as one of the sentences above, will work sufficiently for beginning paragraph development and can always be reworded or polished later.

4.5 Brainstorming Supporting Information

After determining the exact perspective on the subject, supporting material must be identified. Again, brainstorming helps generate ideas for **supporting points** and **supporting details**. Supporting points are the facts given in primary support of the contention in the topic sentence. Supporting details add further information and explanation to the supporting points. If the writer does not have enough knowledge about the subject to write a well-developed composition, he or she will need to do research. As the research progresses, the writer should evaluate whether the chosen contention is supportable and interesting. If not, he should change topic or perspective. The final selection of supporting material is made based on how well it fits the perspective and topic. Only the strongest, most pertinent supporting information should be utilized.

Supporting points are facts given in support of a contention.

4.6 Planning Outline

The organization of ideas into standard outline form is an important skill to master. An outline forces the writer to arrange the supporting information logically and ultimately simplifies writing the paragraph. Outlines can fall into two general forms: (1) key words or phrases, and (2) sentences. If creating standard outlines has not been mastered by now, the student would do well to use other available resources to learn this skill.

Supporting details add additional information to the supporting points.

4B - Example Planning Outline

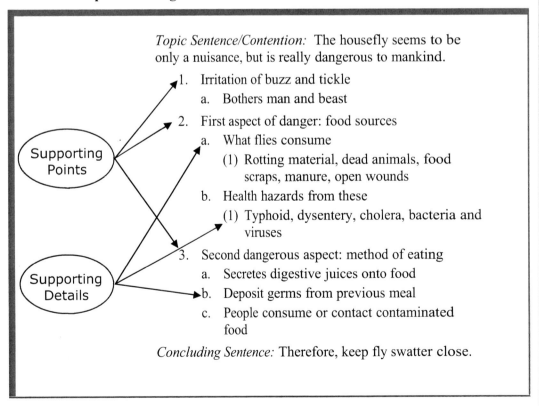

Topic Sentence/Contention: The housefly seems to be only a nuisance, but is really dangerous to mankind.

1. Irritation of buzz and tickle
    a. Bothers man and beast
2. First aspect of danger: food sources
    a. What flies consume
        (1) Rotting material, dead animals, food scraps, manure, open wounds
    b. Health hazards from these
        (1) Typhoid, dysentery, cholera, bacteria and viruses
3. Second dangerous aspect: method of eating
    a. Secretes digestive juices onto food
    b. Deposit germs from previous meal
    c. People consume or contact contaminated food

Concluding Sentence: Therefore, keep fly swatter close.

Illustration 4B above shows the planning outline for the housefly paragraph in the previous lesson (page 21). Several key features within the illustration ought to be present in any well-developed paragraph outline. First, comes the logical and clear topic sentence, complete and in near final form. Below the topic sentence appear the supporting points *(represented by the numbers 1., 2., and 3. in 4B)* and supporting details *(represented by the letters a., b., and c. in 4B)*. Students should always insert into their outlines several supporting details for each supporting point. Finally, an appealing concluding idea ends the outline. When all of these components exist, the actual writing of the paragraph becomes easy. The writer simply converts the ideas into complete sentences and then polishes the paragraph with transitional phrasing, descriptive wording, and varied sentence structure.

Student writers most often fail to adequately explain their supporting points through the use of supporting details. Illustration 4C contains the same "housefly" paragraph written without many of the supporting details as some students might write it. The lack of interesting and convincing supporting detail makes an obvious difference. Any reader would ask several questions: "Precisely, how does the housefly pick up diseases?" "What are the specific sources?" "How, exactly, does the housefly spread the germs?" "What diseases could the housefly spread?" "Is the housefly really a danger to humans?" Overall, the resulting paragraph is boring and unconvincing.

> *Supporting details answer the "what," "how," and "why" questions regarding any contention.*

4C - Under-Developed Outline and Under-Developed Paragraph

Topic Sentence/Contention: The housefly seems to be only a nuisance, but is really dangerous to mankind.

1. It irritates
2. Eats rotten food
3. Spread germs

Concluding Sentence: Therefore, keep fly swatter close.

Upon first glance, the pesky housefly seems to be only a nuisance; however, the insect is actually quite dangerous to mankind. With an irritating buzz and tickle, the housefly bothers man and beast alike. Along with annoying people, the common fly also presents a danger to humans. It eats rotten food full of diseases. Then, wherever the fly lands, it spreads these dangerous germs. Therefore, a fly swatter should be kept close at hand.

Supporting details are essential components of an outline. They comprise the evidence, analysis, and explanation for each supporting point which, in turn, confirms the contention in the topic sentence. Generally, no outline should be considered well-developed without several supporting details under each point. They answer the "what," "how," and "why" questions for the reader and provide interesting nuggets of information. Most importantly, they add persuasiveness to one's argument. The secret to a strong and well-developed paragraph is a fully-developed outline that includes plenty of supporting detail.

4.7 Formalize Topic Sentence

With research completed and supporting information organized into an outline, the writer drafts a more complete topic sentence which indicates the exact purpose of the paragraph. Naturally, this sentence may still be reworded again later to make it more interesting or exact. The purpose that it sets forth, however, must continue to remain consistent with the content.

4.8 Rough Draft

At this point, writing the paragraph should be a simple process. The ideas just need to be communicated in complete sentences in the order that they appear in the planning outline. Also, transitional phrases, explained in the next lesson, will be needed to help the sentences connect into a single unit of thought. Finally, a concluding sentence will complete the paragraph.

4.9 Edit, Polish, Final Draft

The most frequently ignored steps in the writing process are those of editing and polishing. However, these steps are a must in order to produce an excellent piece of writing. It is only after the ideas are drafted that they can be properly considered in light of guidelines for clear thought, structure, and style. Enlisting the assistance of someone else to read the composition at this point can be particularly beneficial in determining if ideas have been clearly communicated in the exact manner desired. If not, it is time to rewrite those areas that need improvement. Editing and polishing will likely take the most time. There can be no shortcut in this process. Editing a paragraph may require numerous rewrites. The willingness to work at revising and improving one's writing will be true evidence of the character of the composer.

Paragraph Process:
1. *Consider*
   - *Topic*
   - *Purpose*
   - *Audience*
2. *Approach*
3. *Preliminary Topic Sentence*
4. *Supporting Information*
5. *Planning Outline*
6. *Formalize Topic Sentence*
7. *Rough Draft*
8. *Edit, Polish, Final Draft*

WEEK 4
The Writing Process Overview

Daily Assignments

────── **Day 1** ──────

A. Reading Assignment:
Read the Week 4 Lesson carefully, paying attention to the steps for developing a paragraph and making certain that you understand the basic form of an outline.

B. Grammar Drill:
1. Drill the state of being verbs and helping verbs again.

2. Rewrite the following sentence in active voice.

Her food was prepared by the chef.

C. Sentence Drill:
Rewrite the following sentence, placing the italicized word(s) in the most emphatic location.

The youngster drove the remote control car to the edge of the table; sadly, it fell to the floor and *broke* when he pushed the accelerator.

D. Lesson Exercise:
Answer the following questions in complete sentences.

1. What three preliminary considerations must be clear before one begins writing any composition?
2. Knowing the audience will influence what four aspects of one's writing?
3. What is brainstorming?
4. What serves as the plan for a formal writing project?

E. Writing Exercise:
Read the sample paragraph below and write a planning outline for it. Your outline should follow the format of the sample on page 29 and include:
- *The <u>topic sentence</u>,*
- *The <u>supporting points</u> (the three areas under repair)*
- *Any additional <u>supporting details</u>, and*
- *The <u>concluding sentence.</u>*

    The Barrett family home is clearly in the midst of a remodel. Initial observations of the outside quickly reveal this fact to any visitor. Siding on the front of the house has yet to be applied, and the logo from the house wrap greets passersby. Windows still need trim pieces, and part of the wood on the front of the house lacks primer or paint. Where the owners hope to one day hang a garage door, a blue tarp hangs across the carport opening. Sturdy posts, which brace the new porch roof, also await trim and finish work. Stepping across the threshold into the living room, one sees changes in this room as well. Two walls display new sheet rock covered with spots of plaster mud which is in the process of being sanded. The pair of new windows in this room await trim boards while manufacturing stickers still adhere to the glass. Down the hallway, one sees a third area of revision. A family room door stands with a symmetrical hole awaiting the installation of a doorknob. In contrast to all the other stain-finished doors down the hallway, this door stands stark and blond with neither stain nor paint. Also in this room, a layer of paint primer covers the recently replaced wall board. Cut away from around the newly installed wood stove, the old carpet begs to be replaced. Evidence in a number of areas seems to suggest that this "vintage" home is undergoing a degree of metamorphosis.

Day 2

A. Grammar Drill:
Drill the first and second columns of prepositions.

B. Sentence Drill:
Identify the structural type of this sentence:

Many Americans have come to understand the significance of their country's history.

C. Formality Drill:
Using the formality and grammar rules explained in Lesson 2, rewrite the sentence below in proper form:

He'll be moving to the desk next to the copy machine.

D. Writing Exercise:
Read the sample paragraph below and write a planning outline for it. Your outline should follow the format of the sample on page 29 and include:
- *The <u>topic sentence</u>,*
- *The <u>supporting points</u> (the budgetary categories)*
- *Any additional <u>supporting details</u>, and*
- *The <u>concluding sentence.</u>*

  Planning a reception for a special event will most likely revolve around budgetary limitations. Securing a location will be the first challenge as it can be expensive to rent a facility that is appropriate in size and formality. The availability of kitchen appliances and other equipment also affect the cost of the location. A second category of expense involves creating the desired atmosphere. What decorations are needed? Is music desired? If so, shall musicians be hired or will pre-recorded music suffice? A third and large area of expense can be food and drink. Some choose to have a sit-down dinner while others may opt for light snacks or desserts. Catering will add to the cost, but may be appropriate for formal settings and large parties. Otherwise, some savings can be gained by those hosting the event preparing the food. Invitations or announcements comprise a final and smaller expense. Numerous companies offer pre-printed invitations which can be ordered. A money saving option might be to purchase blank invitation cards and print them on a computer or write out the invitation by hand. Regardless of the type of reception, these four major areas of expense must be worked into the budget.

Day 3

A. Grammar Drill:
Drill the first and second columns of prepositions.

B. Sentence Drill:
Identify the structural type of this sentence:

Two areas of challenge face the individual who is building his own home: money and time.

C. Formality Drill:
Using the formality and grammar rules explained in Lesson 2, rewrite the sentence below in proper form:

Because John will work diligently.

D. Writing Exercise:
Read the sample paragraph below and write a planning outline for it. Your outline should follow the format of the sample on page 29 and include:
- The <u>topic sentence</u>,
- The <u>supporting points</u> (the areas of comparison)
- Any additional <u>supporting details</u>, and
- The <u>concluding sentence.</u>

    In a number of areas, leaving home to join the military may not be all that different than living at home for the average young person. For example, parents often require appropriate attire depending on the occasion. Certain clothes will be designated for play, other clothes for school, and dress clothes for formal occasions. Likewise, in the military, clothing choices are dictated much of the time. The soldier will be told what clothes to wear for training, when to don his battle fatigues, and what formal occasions require a dress uniform. Another parallel between life at home and in the military is the establishment of standard mealtimes. In both settings, but particularly in the military, meals will be served on a specific schedule, and an individual must be present in order to eat. Curfews are also established at home and in the armed services. In order to maintain productivity and safety on the part of the young person, parents establish times for rising, bedtimes, and limits for staying out. Similarly, the military will dictate when the soldier must be in the barracks and the time for lights out. Chores are an additional requirement in both settings. Child and soldier alike might be required to scrub the bathroom, work in the kitchen, sweep, mop, make beds, do laundry, and run errands. Finally, discipline is a very significant parallel between home and military life. In both arenas, if one does not do as told, he can find himself in significant trouble. The child may be grounded, find himself doing extra chores, or even more serious consequences. Military discipline, which can be more severe, ranges from physical exercise to loss of privileges, to fines, to court marshal. Given these significant parallels between home life and military life, one wonders why so many young people join the military to get away from the restrictions at home.

Put That In Writing 35

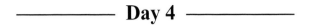
Day 4

A. Grammar Drill:
Drill the first and second columns of prepositions.

B. Sentence Drill:
Identify the structural type of this sentence:

The Arizona of today is far from the setting of the Old West.

C. Formality Drill:
Using the formality and grammar rules explained in Lesson 2, rewrite the sentence below in proper form:

In spite of the fact that settlers there had to be tough as shoe leather, Arizonans built a modern culture in a dry, arid land.

D. Writing Exercise:
Read the sample paragraph below and write a planning outline for it. Your outline should follow the format of the sample on page 29 and include:
- The <u>topic sentence</u>,
- The <u>supporting points</u> (the five major steps in the described process)
- Any additional <u>supporting details</u>, and
- The <u>concluding sentence.</u>

Quilters follow a standard process for assembling quilts. First comes preparation for assembly. The quilt top and backing must be created, and the batting should be chosen. Then the assembly of the layers takes place. A backing fabric layer is laid completely flat on a large surface or stretched onto a quilting frame. One must be certain that the fabric is placed with right side down. Next, the batting material is laid over this backing covering it from edge to edge. Now, the quilt top is accurately placed, right side up, over the back and batting. At this point, the "quilt sandwich" must be temporarily secured together so they will not shift when the final quilting is being done. A number of options may be used for this task. Some quilters apply a quilter's spray adhesive to the back side of the fabrics as the layers are compiled. Others use safety pins, hand basting, or machine basting at this point, to firmly fix the layers. Once all layers have been temporarily compiled, it is time to permanently secure the quilt. This is done by either tying yarns inserted through the layers, or quilting by hand or machine. Basting or temporary fasteners should then be removed. The final step is to finish the edges. The quilter may simply choose to fold the edges of top and back under and stitch along the edge by hand or machine. For fancier edges, one might add bias trim, piping, braiding, or decorative machine stitches. While numerous options exist within the process, assembly of all quilts follows this standard pattern.

Day 5

A. Grammar Drill:
Drill the first and second columns of prepositions.

B. Sentence Drill:
Identify the structural type of this sentence:

Once a haven for people with severe allergies, Phoenix, Arizona, has been filled with so many non-native plants that those sensitive to pollen may now actually find it quite difficult to live there.

C. Formality Drill:
Using the formality and grammar rules explained in Lesson 2, rewrite the sentence below in proper form:

Caught the ball.

D. Writing Exercise:
1. *Brainstorm the topic of your family automobile and decide on an approach or a perspective (as explained on pages 27-28). Develop three strong supporting points. Refer to Illustration 4A if you need help with ideas. This paragraph is to be informative; however, the student may not create a comparison paragraph at this time. This will be introduced in Week 20.*

2. *Develop a topic sentence for your family automobile paragraph, which expresses your perspective (approach), and create a planning outline. Add supporting details under each supporting point. Remember that all paragraphs in the course are to be written in third person. (See page 10.)*

3. *Brainstorming work and planning outline are to be submitted to the instructor on this day.*

WEEK 5

Lesson: *Paragraph Basics 1*

5.1 Introduction

In order to understand the basics of paragraphs, a brief analogy, which could apply to paragraphs, essays, research papers, and even books, might be helpful. Imagine if you will that your teacher was able, with the snap of the fingers, to separate the students' skeletons from their flesh and stand the skeletons against one wall and line up the flesh along the opposite wall. We might say that these represent the basic components of a standard paragraph.

The skeletons would represent the structure. Without flesh on them, they would all appear fairly similar having few obvious differences. Some might be taller, some might have finer bones, and some larger feet than others, yet they would all look quite like one another. This is how essays of various writers would look if we viewed just the structures. Like a skeleton, every standard essay should contain certain components which appear in all other essays.

Let us now look at the flesh resting along the other wall. Compared to the skeletons, each lump of flesh would exhibit numerous distinct differences from the next. Obvious variations in hair, eyes, skin tone, and shape would make it easy to distinguish one individual from another. These lumps of flesh might represent the development and individual style of each paragraph or essay. Like the unique differences between the lumps of flesh, it is easy to see that some compositions have more flair than others, some employ unique wording while others are more plain, and some have more developed ideas.

This analogy can be taken further. Just as flesh with the skeleton snatched away will collapse into a jumble of eyes, hair, arms, and legs, so stylish words become a confusion of ideas apart from standard essay structure. Someone may look at the pile of flesh and say, "What beautiful blue eyes!" Yet one could reply that the eyes would be more beautiful if they were in their proper place on the skeleton rather than atop a limp pile of flesh. So it is with writing. Clever words and phrases fall short if proper form is not followed. One must first create the skeleton (structure), then creatively cover the skeleton with flesh (style) in such a manner that the skeleton is hardly noticed. In order to master the combining of structure and style, both must be clearly understood.

5.2 Paragraph Structure - the "Skeleton"

Writing structure must be mastered before one progresses to style. It provides the skeleton whereby masterfully crafted phrases can be enjoyed.

A. *Topic Sentence*

When following standard paragraph form, the first sentence is the **topic sentence**. As such, it establishes the exact subject of the paragraph. It can be

> *The topic sentence establishes the exact topic, grabs the reader's interest, and sets the tone.*

said that the topic sentence is limiting or binding in that the content of the paragraph will be limited to the bounds set by it. Writers must understand that the topic sentence dictates what will be included in the paragraph, and that all information presented must be **topical** in order for the paragraph to be proper.

In addition to establishing the exact topic of a paragraph, a topic sentence serves **to grab the reader's interest** and **to set the tone for the paragraph**. Therefore, inventive writers strive to word this sentence in such a way that the reader desires more about the topic. Specific tone can be easily established by the choice of wording. For example, if the paragraph is to be a humorous one, the topic sentence will give the reader an indication of such. If the paragraph is to be persuasive, the topic sentence will indicate the writer's position. Clear thinking, mastery of wording, and a well-developed vocabulary will enable the writer to create a topic sentence which accomplishes all three of the above purposes.

B. *Supporting Information*

Once a strong topic sentence is established, it becomes the job of the writer to give sufficient evidence to prove the topic sentence to be true. The evidence chosen by the author is said to make up the **content** of the paragraph because it supports the contention established in the topic sentence. A common mistake is to include information in a paragraph that does not support the contention. For instance, the topic sentence might be, "Dogs make great pets for many reasons." The paragraph would not discuss reasons why a dog is a better pet than a bird or a cat. Doing so would be moving to another topic not covered by the topic sentence. To stay on topic, only positive reasons why a dog makes a great pet would be presented. It is very important that the writer understand exactly the position established by the topic sentence and uses only supporting information in the paragraph that serves to prove that position.

> *Coordinate ideas support the same idea and are at the same level in an outline.*

Supporting information must also be organized into a logical presentation. Without a doubt, the best way to arrive at a logical arrangement of the information is to write out a planning outline. It forces one to arrange the supporting information into coordinate and subordinate positions. Simply put, points in an outline which are equal with each other are called **coordinate ideas** and should appear at the same level within the outline. On the other hand, points that support other points are called **subordinate ideas** to indicate that they come under other points within the outline. The outline form permits a writer to visualize whether an idea is placed at the proper level and under the exact point it is intended to support. (Refer to the illustrated outline in Week 5 Addendum on page 40.) Understanding which ideas are coordinate with each other and which should be subordinate helps the writer remain both logical and on topic.

> *Subordinate ideas come under and support other points in an outline.*

C. *Transitions*

In order to keep the reader moving along and connecting one idea with another, a writer uses **transitional words** or phrases so that the paragraph or essay flows and does not seem choppy. A transition can either tie a point to the previous idea, or signal a change to a new idea. In either case, transitional wording prepares the reader to receive the next piece of information and form a mental outline of the paragraph. Chart 5A lists some of the most commonly used transition words and phrases.

5A - Common Transition Words

after	in order that	until
although	once	when
as	provided that	whenever
because	rather than	where
before	since	whereas
even though	though	wherever
if...then	unless	while

Transition words, phrases, and sentences help ideas in a paragraph flow smoothly.

Well-written paragraphs also contain **transition sentences** to introduce each new supporting point before it is discussed. Transition sentences only establish the next topic for discussion and do not give any supporting details about the point. The writer then discusses the point in the next few sentences before using another transition sentence to introduce the next point. Just like transitional words and phrases, the transitional sentence makes reading flow smoothly, guiding the reader from point to point. In the Week 5 Addendum on the next page, one can see that supporting points 1, 2, and 3 in the planning outline become the transitional sentences in the paragraph and the paragraph outline. The supporting details form the basis of the discussion sentences following each transitional sentence. The student should learn to introduce each point in this manner in order to produce a well-structured paragraph.

D. *Concluding Sentence*

Finally, a standard paragraph contains a **concluding sentence** which restates the topic sentence or summarizes the content of the paragraph using new and interesting words. It might also appeal to the reader to agree with the writer or to take action, especially if the paragraph is designed to be persuasive. The writer must be careful, however, to avoid introducing a new topic, moving to a new contention, or offering exaggeration.

A concluding sentence, which summarizes content or offers an appeal, is the last sentence of a paragraph.

Summary: *Clearly, the characters in <u>The Chronicles of Narnia</u> connect the reader to this fictional land.*

Appeal to reader: *To meet some interesting characters, all should read <u>The Chronicles of Narnia</u>.*

ADDENDUM - WEEK 5
Demonstrating Paragraph Structure
Planning Outline

Topic sentence: A trip to neighborhood like a trip to forest.

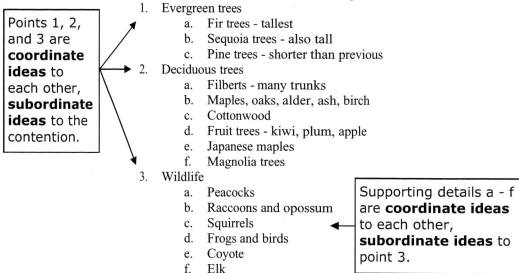

1. Evergreen trees
   a. Fir trees - tallest
   b. Sequoia trees - also tall
   c. Pine trees - shorter than previous
2. Deciduous trees
   a. Filberts - many trunks
   b. Maples, oaks, alder, ash, birch
   c. Cottonwood
   d. Fruit trees - kiwi, plum, apple
   e. Japanese maples
   f. Magnolia trees
3. Wildlife
   a. Peacocks
   b. Raccoons and opossum
   c. Squirrels
   d. Frogs and birds
   e. Coyote
   f. Elk

Points 1, 2, and 3 are **coordinate ideas** to each other, **subordinate ideas** to the contention.

Supporting details a - f are **coordinate ideas** to each other, **subordinate ideas** to point 3.

Concluding sentence: This setting is so enjoyable...

Here is a sample paragraph drawn from the above outline:

  Although the Barretts live in the city, a visit to their neighborhood is like a trip to the forest. Needle bearing trees form the outer canopy of the visual feast of green. Majestically standing guard over the neighborhood, fir trees, seventy-five to one hundred feet tall, make up the framework of the greenery that fills the neighborhood. Among these fir trees, an occasional sequoia rises to compete with the firs for sunlight and height. Completing the evergreen varieties are pine trees which seem dwarfed by the larger evergreens. In addition to all of this greenery, an abundance of deciduous trees fills any spaces which have not been cleared by home owners. Filbert trees, since this was once a filbert orchard, are most in abundance. Their many-branched trunks allow the trees to spread out on all sides, like a floral arrangement. Sugar maples, oaks, alder, ash, and birch trees add their beautiful foliage. Even a few cottonwood trees ascend in vertical motion. Here and there fruit trees also thrive. Some of these trees, such as kiwi and plum, have been planted by home owners, but it seems that a few apple trees have just naturally sprung up from seeds. Japanese maples, red and green, fill many of the front yards along the street, creating a rippled, lacy look and a stunning splash of color across the green canvas. Offering its tulip-shaped flowers, an occasional magnolia tree delights onlookers. To complete the feeling of a trip to the forest is the daily encounter with wildlife. The most colorful are the wild peacocks which parade daily up and down the street calling to one another with raucous honks and screeches. Raccoons and opossums make routine evening rounds in search of food and frolic. Like speeding over an intricate freeway system, squirrels traverse the overhead power lines, hardly pausing to change routes or chatter at a passerby. Off in the distance, frogs croak with a regular cadence, and numerous types of birds flit from tree to tree. An occasional coyote trots down the paved road trying to decide if it is in the city or the woods. Even a full grown elk with a majestic set of antlers has recently made himself at home. This setting is so enjoyable that a slow drive down the Barretts' street can seem like a trip away from the city.

Coordinating and subordinating information in paragraphs should be presented so logically that the paragraph itself can actually fall into a well written outline. Such an outline comes easily from the above paragraph.

<u>T.S.</u>: Although the Barretts live in the city, a visit to their neighborhood is like a trip to the forest.
1. Needle bearing trees form the outer canopy of the visual feast of green.
    a. Majestically standing guard over the neighborhood, fir trees, seventy-five to one hundred feet tall, make up the framework of the greenery that fills the neighborhood.
    b. Among these fir trees, an occasional sequoia rises to compete with the firs for sunlight and height.
    c. Completing the evergreen varieties are pine trees which seem dwarfed by the larger evergreens.
2. In addition to all of this greenery, an abundance of deciduous trees fills any spaces which have not been cleared by home owners.
    a. Filbert trees, since this was once a filbert orchard, are most in abundance.
        (1) Their many branched trunks allow the trees to spread out on all sides, like a floral arrangement.
    b. Sugar maples, oaks, alder, ash, and birch trees add their beautiful foliage.
    c. Even a few cottonwood trees ascend in vertical motion.
    d. Here and there fruit trees also thrive.
        (1) Some of these trees, such as kiwi and plum, have been planted by home owners, but it seems that a few apple trees have just naturally sprung up from seeds.
    e. Japanese maples, red and green, fill many of the front yards along the street, creating a rippled, lacy look and a stunning splash of color across the green canvas.
    f. Offering its tulip-shaped flowers, an occasional magnolia tree delights onlookers.
3. To complete the feeling of a trip to the forest is the daily encounter with wildlife.
    a. The most colorful are the wild peacocks which parade daily up and down the street calling to one another with raucous honks and screeches.
    b. Raccoons and opossums make routine evening rounds in search of food and frolic.
    c. Like speeding over an intricate freeway system, squirrels traverse the overhead power lines hardly pausing to change routes or chatter at a passerby.
    d. Off in the distance frogs croak with a regular cadence, and numerous types of birds flit from tree to tree.
    e. An occasional coyote trots down the paved road trying to decide if it is in the city or the woods.
    f. Even a full grown elk with a majestic set of antlers has recently made himself at home.

<u>C.S.</u>: This setting is so enjoyable that a slow drive down the Barretts' street can seem like a trip away from the city.

WEEK 5
Paragraph Basics 1

Daily Assignments

—————— Day 1 ——————

A. Reading Assignment:
Read the Week 5 Lesson carefully, taking time to understand each concept.

B. Grammar Drill:
Rewrite the following sentence in active voice.

The visitors were guided through the museum by the curator.

C. Sentence Drill:
Rewrite the following sentence, placing the italicized word(s) in the most emphatic location.

The *visitors* were guided through the museum by the curator.

D. Lesson Exercise:
Answer the following questions in complete sentences.

1. What are the four basic components of any standard paragraph?
2. What are the three purposes of the topic sentence?
3. Explain the difference between coordinate and subordinate ideas.
4. Why are transitions important?
5. What is a concluding sentence supposed to do?

E. Writing Exercise:
1. Read the sample paragraph below. Identify the <u>topic sentence</u>, <u>supporting points</u>, <u>supporting details</u>, and <u>conclusion</u>. Write these points in planning outline form.

> Americans celebrate the Fourth of July holiday with various traditional activities. Decorating with red, white, and blue creates an atmosphere of anticipation for the holiday. Flags and flag themes are displayed on fences, flag poles, and even automobiles. If the weather is pleasant, outdoor activities are generally planned. Numerous games, such as volleyball, baseball, Frisbee®, and Hacky Sack®, entertain the younger generation. Older folks may sit and watch the youngsters' activity, or they may join in a genteel game of croquet. Feasting on food is also a primary focus of the day. Many Americans choose to barbecue meat of some sort. They also add to this delightful salads, fresh fruits, and even home made ice cream. As far as traditions go, Americans hold firmly to their grand finale: fireworks. Some fireworks may be purchased by the families and lighted at their homes. Other, larger displays, are presented by cities around the country. For viewing these, families simply travel to an appropriate vantage point, set up lawn chairs, snuggle under warm blankets, and watch the colorful explosions in the sky. Whether the fireworks are done at a home or in a larger area, the bright lights and dazzling sparkles are certain to bring "oohs" and "aahs" from the onlookers. Truly, simple traditions make the Fourth of July a special holiday for Americans.

Put That In Writing 43

2. Rewrite the above paragraph, arranging each sentence in outline form. Refer to the sentence outline example in Week 5 Addendum on page 41.

3. Underline all transitional words and phrases. Notice how the writer uses them to create a smooth change from discussion of one point to the next.

———— Day 2 ————

A. Grammar Drill:
Continue to drill the prepositions you have studied thus far.

B. Sentence Drill:
Identify the structural type of this sentence:

John and Charles Wesley, who grew up in an Anglican home, became two of the most prominent ministers in England and America during the 1700's.

C. Formality Drill:
Using the formality and grammar rules explained in Lesson 2, rewrite the sentence below in proper form:

John Wesley's sermons, which are still published today, were worth reading.

D. Writing Exercise*:
Over the next few days, you will begin writing a paragraph about your family automobile using the topic sentence and outline developed on Day 5 of Week 4, drafting a few sentences at a time. On a separate sheet of paper, perform the following steps:

1. Write your topic sentence. Remember to use third person throughout the paragraph.
2. Introduce your first point about the family automobile using a transition word or phrase to begin the first sentence.
3. Write two or more sentences discussing this first point. These two sentences could actually be sub-points to the major point or further explanation and examples of the main point. Save today's work for submission on Day 5.

* *Proper formatting of paragraphs must be followed throughout this course. Thus, you will follow these guidelines from this point on:*
   a. Double-space
   b. 1 inch margins
   c. 12 point, standard font
   d. Proper heading on first page

———— Day 3 ————

A. Grammar Drill:
Continue to drill the prepositions you have studied thus far.

B. Sentence Drill:
Identify the structural type of this sentence:

Charles Wesley is most remembered for the many hymns which he wrote, and these hymns are still sung in churches today.

C. Formality Drill:
Using the formality and grammar rules explained in Lesson 2, rewrite the sentence below in proper form:

The Wesleys took so much flack over their message that one might wonder why they did not give up preaching.

D. Writing Exercise:
Continue developing your paragraph begun yesterday with the following steps:

1. Introduce your second point with a transition word or phrase leading the sentence.
2. Write two or more sentences discussing this second major point. Again, these two sentences may be sub-points, further explanation, or examples of your second point.
3. Save today's paper for submission on Day 5.

Day 4

A. Grammar Drill:
Continue to drill the prepositions you have studied thus far.

B. Sentence Drill:
Identify the structural type of this sentence:

Niccolo Machiavelli wrote *The Prince*, which espoused his theories of government.

C. Formality Drill:
Using the formality and grammar rules explained in Lesson 2, rewrite the sentence below in proper form:

The book, *Gulliver's Travels,* was written by Jonathan Swift.

D. Writing Exercise:
Continue developing your paragraph by completing the following steps:

1. With a final transition word or phrase, introduce your third point.
2. Again, explain or give examples which support your third point.
3. Again, save this work to submit on Day 5.

Day 5

A. Grammar Drill:
Continue to drill the prepositions you have studied thus far.

B. Sentence Drill:
Identify the structural type of this sentence:

Jonathan Swift wrote satire in response to the European Enlightenment, and Benjamin Franklin wrote satire in response to the King of England, Charles III.

C. Formality Drill:
Using the formality and grammar rules explained in Lesson 2, rewrite the sentence below in proper form:

Franklin, who wrote prolifically, was smart as a whip.

D. Writing Exercise:
1. *Complete your paragraph on the family automobile by doing the following:*
   a. Write a concluding sentence which summarizes your general contention. Create a copy of your complete paragraph before you begin to edit. Submit this draft with your finished paragraph.
   b. Now edit your paragraph. Mark errors and changes.
      o Did you follow the writing rules studied in Week 2?
      o Is all content on topic?
      o Is the most important information located at points of strongest emphasis in the sentences?
      o Is each new supporting point introduced with a transition?
   c. Re-write a final draft of your paragraph.

2. *Submit your work to the instructor:*
   a. Final draft paragraph
   b. Daily drafts
   c. Planning outline
   d. Brainstorming

WEEK 6
Paragraph Basics 1 (continued)

Daily Assignments
The exercises for Week 6 are based on the Lessons from Weeks 4 & 5.

> From this point forward, if you are writing your assignments on a computer, print each day's work for submission with final draft on Day 5.

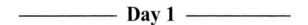

Day 1

A. Reading Assignment:
Read again the Lessons from Weeks 4 and 5 to be certain that you understand the writing process and the desired end product.

B. Grammar Drill:
1. Drill the state of being verbs and helping verbs again.
2. Rewrite the following sentence in active voice.

   Her situation was controlled by outside forces.

C. Sentence Drill:
Rewrite the following sentence placing the italicized word(s) in the most emphatic location.

She collapsed to the ground *in fright* after the narrow escape.

D. Lesson Exercise:
Answer the following questions based on material in the lessons from Weeks 4 and 5 in complete sentences.

1. Based on the Week 4 Lesson, list the six steps which precede the creation of a rough draft.
2. What are the three purposes of a topic sentence?
3. What, besides a restatement or summary, may comprise a concluding sentence?
4. What common error do writers make when presenting supporting information?

E. Writing Exercise:
This week you will develop a paragraph on the topic of yard care, utilizing the following list of brainstorming ideas. If you know other ideas that will enhance the topic, add them to the list. Then follow steps 1 through 3 to start your paragraph.

lawn	water	trimming/pruning
types of grasses	sprinkler	fertilizing
shrubs/bushes	sprinkler system	edging
flowers	pest control	trees
bulbs	fungus control	de-thatching
seeds	weed control	mowing

1. Brainstorm a topic sentence for a paragraph, contending that a well-kept yard requires much work.

    Purpose: inform
    Audience: prospective first-time homeowner

2. Choose three main categories or supporting points which can serve as evidence of your contention, and organize them into a planning outline; add supporting details.

3. Write your brainstorming list and planning outline neatly, in a manner suitable for submission with your final draft.

Day 2

A. Grammar Drill:
Drill the first two columns of prepositions and add the third column to your drill.

B. Sentence Drill:
Identify the structural type of this sentence:

The Federalist is a compilation of essays expressing favoritism toward the proposed United States Constitution; however, in response to proponents of a strong central government, the Anti-Federalists published a compilation of opposing essays.

C. Formality Drill:
Using the formality and grammar rules explained in Lesson 2, rewrite the sentence below in proper form:

Alexis de Tocqueville and his colleague, Gustave de Beaumont, traveled throughout the eastern United States analyzing American culture and democracy; he subsequently published a book on their findings.

D. Writing Exercise:
Begin your yard care paragraph by copying your topic sentence from your planning outline. Next, write a transitional sentence to introduce your first point. Finally, write three or more sentences discussing the details supporting your first point.

Day 3

A. Grammar Drill:
Drill the prepositions through column three.

B. Sentence Drill:
Identify the structural type of this sentence:

Tocqueville was from France where many had suffered under tyrannical rule, and he endeavored to understand what made a free society work.

C. Formality Drill:
Using the formality and grammar rules explained in Lesson 2, rewrite the sentence below in proper form:

Tocqueville hung out in America in order to observe the American people and their political system.

D. Writing Exercise:
Introduce your second point about the hard work of yard care with a transition, such as those listed in Chart 5A on page 39, then write two or more sentences discussing this second major point. Again, these two sentences should help show how your second main point proves that a well-kept yard takes much work.

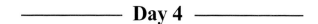

— Day 4 —

A. Grammar Drill:
Drill the list of prepositions through column three.

B. Sentence Drill:
Identify the structural type of this sentence:

Tocqueville observed that religion played a primary role in making America great.

C. Formality Drill:
Using the formality and grammar rules explained in Lesson 2, rewrite the sentences below in proper form:

The new employee was as nervous as a long-tailed cat in a room full of rocking chairs.

D. Writing Exercise:
With a final transition word or phrase, add your third point to your paragraph. Again, explain or give examples which support this point and tie it to the topic.

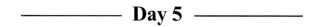

— Day 5 —

A. Grammar Drill:
Again, drill the list of prepositions through column three.

B. Sentence Drill:
Identify the structural type of this sentence:

From the job description he was given, the newly hired janitor knew that he would be kept busy each and every day.

C. Formality Drill:
Using the formality and grammar rules explained in Lesson 2, rewrite the sentence below in proper form:

Thinking that the problem was solved.

D. Writing Exercise:
Complete your paragraph on yard work by doing the following:

1. Write a concluding sentence which summarizes your general contention. Create a copy of your completed paragraph.
2. Now proceed with editing your paragraph. Mark errors and changes on this draft.
   - Did you follow the writing rules studied in Week 2?
   - Is all content on topic?
   - Is the most important information located at points of strongest emphasis in the sentences?
   - Is each new supporting point introduced with a transition?
3. Re-write a final draft of your paragraph to turn in to your instructor along with the corrected draft, daily drafts, planning outline, and the brainstorming.

Reminder to instructor:

Week 10 will require the use of an encyclopedia and other research books on the solar system, Mark Twain, and George Washington Carver. These resources should be ready for student use on the first day of that week.

WEEK 7

Lesson: *Paragraph Basics 2*

7.1 Introduction

Having studied paragraph structure, it is time to look at the other half of writing well: mastery of style. When one only focuses on structure, the paragraphs produced can be boring and without much variation. Creative writing is desirable. However, students often sacrifice formal writing standards in an attempt to be stylish; this should never be done. In this unit, strategies will be discussed for adding "creative flesh" to an assignment that will not only preserve writing standards, but also produce writing that is clear and interesting to read.

7.2 Paragraph Style - the "Flesh"

A. Sentence Variety

A paragraph should contain a variety of sentence structures, and key words, which support the contention, should be placed in positions of emphasis. Varying sentence structure helps hold the reader's attention and eases reading. In addition, placing the most important information at the end of the sentence gives it the strongest emphasis for the reader. These two skills were discussed in detail in Lesson 1, *Sentence Savvy*.

B. Creative Wording

(1) Specific nouns

Nouns can convey general concepts or pinpoint a specific person, place, or thing. By using specific nouns, a writer creates a more accurate picture in the reader's mind as shown in the following examples:

General Nouns: *The computer proved helpful in his study.*

Specific Nouns: *The encyclopedia software proved helpful in his study of photosynthesis.*

(2) Colorful action verbs

Using verbs that show action produces stronger writing than using those verbs which show a state of being (am, are, was, were, be, been, being, is). It will not be possible, nor is it the goal, to eliminate all state of being verbs, but single word action verbs will increase the intensity of one's writing.

Weak: *She was on the spinning merry-go-round.*

Better: *She clung tightly to the spinning merry-go-round.*

Also Better: *She spun continuously on the twirling merry-go-round.*

Noun:
a word that names a person, place, thing, or idea.

Verb:
a word that expresses action or state of being

> **Adjectives modify nouns or pronouns and tell: what kind, which one, how many, how much, and whose.**

(3) Precise adjectives and adverbs

Another stylistic priority is the use of precise adjectives and adverbs. The writer should avoid the many overused adjectives which communicate general ideas or emotion, such as: awesome, great, wonderful, very, or really. These do not give the audience a specific impression. One must strive to create an exact picture in the reader's mind by choosing adjectives and adverbs that add accuracy to the message.

General: *Removal of the carpet seemed the only option for the homeowners.*

Precise: *Immediate removal of the damaged, rotting carpet seemed the only option for the discouraged homeowners.*

General: *Atop the dresser sat the lamp, shining light from beneath its shade.*

Precise: *Atop the antique oak dresser sat the gold-gilded lamp which softly dispersed pale light from beneath its fringed shade.*

C. Style Points

(1) Variety of Opening Words

Starting sentences with different opening words is a second way to create variety in the paragraph.

(a) Opening adverb (frequently ending with "ly")

> *Thankfully, his child suffered no injury in the accident.*
> *Carefully, the chef measures out the next ingredient.*
> *Wisely, the son listens to his father's counsel.*

> **Adverbs modify verbs, adjectives, or adverbs and tell: where, when, why, how, how often, and to what extent.**

(b) Opening participle

> *Running, he tripped and fell.*
> *Barking, the dog backed away from the strangers who had entered the yard.*
> *Falling, the young man knew that he had lost the log rolling contest.*

(2) Variety of Opening Phrases

Phrases may also be used to vary sentence openings. A **phrase**, which functions as a part of speech, is a group of words without a subject and verb.

(a) Opening participial phrase

- ***Present participial phrase***

> *Running for his life, he tripped and fell.*
> *Breathing very heavily, Mrs. Jones began to explain the situation.*
> *Crying uncontrollably, the baby begged to be held by its mother.*

> **A phrase is a group of words that functions as a part of speech and contains no subject or verb.**

- **Past participial phrase**

    <u>Finished with his dinner</u>, the boy ran outside to play.
    <u>Chopped down by the lumbermen</u>, the trees were hauled off to the mill.

(b) **Opening prepositional phrase**

- **Prepositional phrases working as adverbs**

    <u>For the sake of the baby monkey</u>, zoo keepers closed the exhibit.
    <u>In the ocean</u>, the whale swam toward freedom.

(c) **Opening infinitive phrase**

Infinitive phrases are usually, but not always, in the form "to + [*verb*]" and work as nouns, adjectives, or adverbs. They are often followed by a prepositional phrase.

Noun: <u>To run</u> in the Hood to Coast relay race is a lifetime goal for many.

Adverb: <u>To see</u> if the store was closed, Lloyd tried to open the front door.

(3) Variety of Clauses

This section expands upon the discussion in Lesson 1 of complex and compound-complex sentences. Just to review, a clause is a cluster of words which contains a subject and a predicate. In some instances clauses stand alone as a sentence. In other situations like those below, the clause is dependent and functions as a part of speech.

(a) **Opening adverbial clause**

An adverbial clause which does the work of an adverb can be a sentence opener.

<u>While the stunned family looked on</u>, the dog jumped to the table and began to devour their breakfast.
<u>Since the dog ate all the scrambled eggs from the plate</u>, breakfast was clearly over.

(b) **Adjective clause**

While not usually working as an opener, the adjective clause breaks up the standard sentence form and adds interest.

The dress, <u>which her mother made</u>, fit perfectly.
The family car, <u>which had been totaled</u>, was hauled away to the junkyard.
Our mother, <u>who had cared for us</u> while we were young, now needed our care.

Participle:
A verb form used as an adjective

Prepositions:
A word that shows a relationship between its object and another word in the sentence.

Infinitive:
The word "to" plus a verb form, functioning as a noun, adjective, or adverb

(4) Altering traditional word order

Standard word order in an English sentence is subject then verb. Reversing this order creates an interesting effect. The technique, however, must be used sparingly, at a few strategic points of emphasis.

Traditional Order: *The car rolled onto the driveway.*

Reversed Order: *Onto the driveway rolled the car.*

Traditional Order: *The choice to remain pure begins in the mind.*

Reversed Order: *In the mind begins the choice to remain pure.*

D. Literary Devices (Techniques)

In addition to the previous options for creativity in writing, one can implement specific literary devices, sometimes called literary terms. These techniques are traditionally practiced in both poetry and prose, and a student will occasionally use such devices without realizing he or she has done so. Master writers, however, view literary devices as tools to be used consciously. The following literary devices are introduced in this course. Each device will be defined and explained in detail along with each assignment.

Analogy	Alliteration
Simile	Parallelism
Metaphor	Hyperbole/Understatement
Personification	Rhetorical question

7.3 Conclusion

Naturally, all of these techniques cannot be used at once. These strategies for adding "flesh" to the "skeleton" can also be likened to tools for a carpenter. Once learned, they are available in the "toolbox," so to speak, so they can be applied at appropriate times to add style and variety. Learning how and when to use each technique will come with the student's conscious effort during the writing exercises in this course. A helpful Style Point Reference List is available in Appendix B.

All the guidelines discussed thus far in this course are summarized in the following checklist. For each paragraph assignment, the student should fill out the check list, making certain all the guidelines have been followed and required style points included, and turn it in with the assignment. A version, ready to photocopy, is located in Appendix C.

Paragraph Checklist

Structure
- ☐ I have a clearly developed outline.
- ☐ I have an accurate and concise topic sentence.
- ☐ All supporting sentences are topical to the topic sentence.
- ☐ My ideas are developed clearly and logically.
- ☐ I have placed subordinate ideas in subordinate construction.
- ☐ I have a proper concluding sentence.

General Guidelines
- ☐ I have eliminated contractions, colloquial wording, slang, and clichés.
- ☐ I have written with the appropriate level of formality.
- ☐ I have eliminated sentence fragments and nominalization.
- ☐ I have placed important ideas at points of emphasis.

Grammatical Guidelines
- ☐ I have corrected all spelling and punctuation errors.
- ☐ I have kept subjects and verbs in agreement.
- ☐ I have kept verb tenses consistent.
- ☐ Antecedents of pronouns are clear.
- ☐ Person and number are consistent.
- ☐ I have written as many sentences as possible in active voice.

Style
- ☐ I have used precise words: adjectives, adverbs, verbs, and nouns.
- ☐ I have varied sentence patterns:
  - simple, compound, complex, compound-complex
  - variety of opening words, phrases, clauses.
  - occasionally altered traditional word order.
- ☐ I have fully developed ideas so the reader understands and pictures my point.
- ☐ I have used transition words and phrases in order to help the reader follow my logic.
- ☐ I have used the literary device assigned.

Style Point Checklist

Style Points — as explained in Week 7, Paragraph Basics 2
- ☐ S1 Opening adverb.
- ☐ S2 Opening participle.
- ☐ S3 Opening participial phrase.
- ☐ S4 Opening prepositional phrase.
- ☐ S5 Opening infinitive phrase.
- ☐ S6 Opening adverbial clause.
- ☐ S7 Adjective clause.
- ☐ S8 Altering traditional word order.

> **Reminder to instructor:**
> Students will be required to use this checklist in Weeks 9, 11, 14, 17, 20, 23, 26, 29, 32, and 35. A copyable master is located in Appendix C on page 201.

WEEK 7
Paragraph Basics 2

Daily Assignments

―――― **Day 1** ――――

A. Reading Assignment:
Read the Week 7 Lesson carefully, taking time to understand each concept.

B. Grammar Drill:
Rewrite the following sentence in active voice.

The cough drop was accidentally swallowed by the dog.

C. Sentence Drill:
Rewrite the following sentence, placing the italicized word(s) in the most emphatic location.

The *cough drop* was accidentally swallowed by the dog.

D. Lesson Exercise:
Answer the following questions in complete sentences.

1. What two parts of speech should be specific and colorful in order to convey an interesting picture to the reader?
2. What do adjectives modify? What standard questions do they answer?
3. What do adverbs modify? What standard questions do they answer?
4. What two, single-word, opening style points does this lesson present?
5. What is the difference between a phrase and a clause?
6. In a complete sentence, list the kinds of opening phrase style points which might be used to create variety in writing.
7. In a complete sentence, list two clause style points, one opener and one non-opener, which might be used to create variety in writing.

E. Style Drill:
Identify the style point used in the following sentence.

Through his writings, Ralph Waldo Emerson promoted his belief in the goodness of every individual.

F. Writing Exercise:
1. *Brainstorm a list of chores and write a planning outline for a paragraph on three selected chores. You should take a perspective on these chores. For example, the chores might be difficult, pleasant, intriguing, disgusting, or rewarding. Once you have determined your contention regarding three chores, create a topic sentence, plan supporting details, and put them into a well-developed planning outline, which may be used in a future assignment.*

   Purpose: inform   Audience: peers

Put That In Writing   57

Example list of chores:

Washing dishes	Clean toilet	Clean oven
Vacuum floors	Wash car	Clean refrigerator
Mop floors	Clean cupboards/closets	Cleaning one's room
Clean bathtub	Dust	Bathe dog

2. *Practice the style points by creating two sentences on topics of your choice, one sentence for each of the following style points:*

   a. Opening participle (page 52)
   b. Opening prepositional phrase (page 53)

Day 2

A. Grammar Drill:
Continue to drill the first three columns of prepositions.

B. Formality Drill:
Using the formality and grammar rules explained in Lesson 2, rewrite the sentence below in proper form:

When Emerson wrote about mankind, he expressed belief that he could transcend previous flaws by his own effort.

C. Style Drill:
Identify the style point used in the following sentence.

Frankly, Emerson's philosophies were a drastic shift from the belief system of his forefathers.

D. Writing Exercise:

1. *Brainstorm a list of departments, products, and services available in an average grocery store. Create a planning outline for a paragraph contending that grocery stores in this country present the consumer with a broad range of choices. Based on this perspective, create a strong topic sentence and develop appropriate supporting information. This planning outline may be used in a future assignment.*

   Purpose: inform   *Audience: immigrant*

   Brainstorming suggestions:

prepared foods/delicatessen	meat	produce	baking supplies
cards/magazines/books	bakery	staples	condiments
milk/cheese/eggs	wine/beverages	frozen food	videos
medicine/pharmacy	canned goods	dairy	plants/flowers
soaps/shampoos			

2. *Practice the style points by creating two sentences on topics of your choice, one sentence for each of the following style points:*

   a. Opening infinitive phrase (page 53)
   b. Adjective clause (page 53-54)

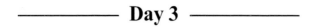

Day 3

A. Grammar Drill:
Continue to rehearse the prepositions you have studied thus far.

B. Formality Drill:
Using the formality and grammar rules explained in Lesson 2, rewrite the sentence below in proper form:

Emerson finally came to the point that he believes the human being to be God.

C. Style Drill:
Identify the style point used in the following sentence.

To express his beliefs, Emerson used poetry and prose filled with all sorts of imagery.

D. Writing Exercise:
1. *Brainstorm a list of favorite vacation destinations in your state. Use a map or tourist guide if you need help. Group them into general categories for discussion in a paragraph. Such categories may include, but are not limited to, water sports destinations, hiking locales, camping spots, scenic areas, easy to access locations, remote regions, and so forth. You determine the categories and list some vacation destinations underneath them. Organize these into a logical outline for a paragraph. The contention should be that your state offers delights for travelers. Using this perspective, create a topic sentence, plan supporting details, and arrange them into a well-developed planning outline. You **may not be able to include all of the ideas you generate**, so it is up to you to determine which ones <u>best</u> make the case for your contention. This planning outline may be used in a future assignment.*

   Purpose: inform
   Audience: tourist considering travel to your state

2. *Practice the style points by creating three sentences on topics of your choice, one sentence for each of the following style points:*

   a. Opening adverbial clause (page 53)
   b. Opening participle (page 52)
   c. Altering traditional word order (page 54)

Day 4

A. Grammar Drill:
Continue to rehearse the first three columns of prepositions.

B. Formality Drill:
Using the formality and grammar rules explained in Lesson 2, rewrite the sentence below in proper form:

I think that Emerson's expressed belief in the "divinity of self" had a significant impact on succeeding generations.

C. Style Drill:
Identify the style point used in the following sentence.

Emerson raises significant questions, which must be considered carefully, regarding the nature of mankind.

D. Writing Exercise:
1. *Brainstorm a list of different categories of music. The goal of this paragraph is to discuss the varieties of music to which Americans listen. This day, you must determine your own contention. Select the musical categories that support your contention and create a topic sentence that expresses your perspective. Organize your supporting points and supporting details into a logical planning outline. Again, this planning outline may be used in a future assignment.*

    Purpose: inform
    Audience: peers

2. *Practice the style points by creating three sentences on topics of your choice, one sentence for each of the following style points:*

    a. Adjective clause (page 53-54)
    b. Opening adverb (page 52)
    c. Opening participial phrase (page 52-53)

Day 5

A. Test:
Complete Week 7 Quiz over Week 5 Lesson: Paragraph Basics 1 and Week 7 Lesson: Paragraph Basics 2.

WEEK 8
Paragraph Basics 2 (continued)

Daily Assignments

――――― **Day 1** ―――――

A. Reading Assignment:
Re-read the Week 7 Lesson carefully, being certain you understand each style point discussed on pages 52-54. Find any terms you do not understand in a grammar handbook.

B. Sentence Drill:
Rewrite the following sentence, placing the italicized word(s) in the most emphatic location.

In effort to win a *prize*, Michael and Ryan threw darts at the target.

C. Style Drill:
Identify the style points used in the following sentences.

1. For centuries, people have debated whether William Shakespeare was an actual person or if his works were written by others under his name.
2. Frankly, most experts believe there are enough facts to establish that Shakespeare actually lived.
3. Coming at the time of the English Renaissance, Shakespeare elevated the use of the English language to new heights.
4. Shakespeare, who by his writing forever changed the world, even invented new words and phrases which are still in use today.
5. For example, Shakespeare first used the phrase "he has eaten me out of house and home" in his play *Henry IV Part 2*.
6. Most parents who use the phrase probably have no idea that they are quoting Shakespeare.
7. To express an inability to understand what was said, one might say, "It was Greek to me," not realizing the phrase is from Shakespeare's play, *Julius Caesar*.
8. Crafting more than just tragedies, Shakespeare wrote a number of comedies.
9. From *The Merry Wives of Windsor* came the saying, "throw cold water on it."
10. When one has eaten too much dessert, he probably does not know that he is quoting from Shakespeare's *As You Like It* by saying he has had "too much of a good thing."

――――― **Day 2** ―――――

A. Grammar Drill:
Continue to rehearse the prepositions you have studied thus far, and add the fourth column to your work.

B. **Formality Drill:**
Using the formality and grammar rules explained in Lesson 2, rewrite the sentence below in proper form:

For a true delight, you should read a Shakespearean comedy. *(Remember that the understood "you" of an imperative sentence does not fix this formality problem.)*

C. **Style Drill:**
Identify the style point used in the following sentence.

Shakespeare, whose first love was acting, created thirty-seven plays, two narrative poems, and 154 sonnets.

D. **Writing Exercise:**
Create four sentences on topics of your choice, each sentence using one of the following style points.

1. Opening adverb (page 52)
2. Opening participle (page 52)
3. Opening participial phrase (page 52-53)
4. Opening prepositional phrase (page 53)

Day 3

A. **Grammar Drill:**
Continue rehearsing the first four columns of prepositions.

B. **Formality Drill:**
Using the formality and grammar rules explained in Lesson 2, rewrite the sentence below in proper form:

You must understand that although Shakespeare's comedies can be tragic, they qualify as comedies because they always culminate in a happy outcome.

C. **Style Drill:**
Identify the two style points used in the following sentence.

To make a statement about solitary confinement, Charles Dickens told, in *A Tale of Two Cities,* of Dr. Manette, whose mental problems stemmed from captivity in isolation.

D. **Writing Exercise:**
Create four sentences on topics of your choice, each sentence using one of the following style points.

1. Opening infinitive phrase (page 53)
2. Opening adverbial clause (page 53)
3. Adjective clause (page 53)
4. Altering traditional word order (page 54)

Day 4

A. Grammar Drill:
Continue to rehearse the prepositions you have studied thus far.

B. Formality Drill:
Using the formality and grammar rules explained in Lesson 2, rewrite the sentence below in proper form:

Charles Dickens' character, Sydney Carton, wasn't a man of principle.

C. Style Drill:
Identify the style point used in the following sentence.

Interestingly, Dickens's characters often seemed to only display a single dimension or trait.

D. Writing Exercise:
Create four sentences on topics of your choice, each sentence using one of the following style points.

1. Opening adverb (page 52)
2. Opening participle (page 52)
3. Opening participial phrase (page 52-53)
4. Opening prepositional phrase (page 53)

Day 5

A. Grammar Drill:
Continue to rehearse the first four columns of prepositions.

B. Formality Drill:
Using the formality and grammar rules explained in Lesson 2, rewrite the sentence below in proper form:

I wonder if Dickens may have portrayed prisons as he did because of the time his father spent in a debtor's prison.

C. Style Drill:
Identify the style point used in the following sentence.

As a prodigal lived Dickens's character, Pip.

D. Writing Exercise:
Create four sentences on topics of your choice, each sentence using one of the following style points.

1. Opening infinitive phrase (page 53)
2. Opening adverbial clause (page 53)
3. Adjective clause (page 53)
4. Altering traditional word order (page 54)

WEEK 9

Descriptive Paragraphs

9.1 Introduction

Descriptive wording can be found in many types of paragraphs; however, the goal of this unit is to teach students to design whole paragraphs with the intent of describing something to the reader. A paragraph written in such a way as to paint a picture in the reader's mind or to give a sense of something the writer is seeing, experiencing, or imagining is said to be a **descriptive paragraph**.

A skillful writer paints a picture for the reader by using interesting nouns, appealing verbs, and well-chosen adjectives and adverbs.

Strong description paints pictures with words.

Plain: *A man stood by the road.*

Descriptive: *An elderly, disheveled man stared longingly into the distance as he leaned against a mailbox along side the road.*

Plain: *The peacock pecked the ground.*

Descriptive: *With quick bobs of its head, a colorful peacock pecked among the leaves for bugs and seeds.*

Plain: *The book was fun to read.*

Descriptive: *The suspenseful novel captured her attention.*

Plain: *She bought the purse.*

Descriptive: *The woman carefully contemplated the vast array of purses before reluctantly purchasing the black one.*

Plain: *Bob made the bed.*

Descriptive: *Bob heaved the blankets over the mattress just far enough to qualify as making the bed but not enough to be called neat.*

9.2 Holding the Reader's Interest

Week 2 Lesson explained that holding the reader's interest with informative writing is a challenge. To increase appeal when writing descriptively, authors will use wording that involves the reader at the level of the senses and emotions. Notice in the above examples that the descriptive words cause the reader to think about how something must look, feel, taste, sound, smell, or evoke an emotion. This technique brings the descriptive paragraph alive in the reader's mind, making it enjoyable and interesting to read.

Appealing to the senses and emotions helps to engage the reader's interest.

9.3 Planning a descriptive paragraph

A sample paragraph about a room will be used to demonstrate the development of a descriptive paragraph. Illustration 9A shows how a planner can be used to record items to describe and relate to various senses and emotions.

9A - Descriptive Paragraph Planner

Topic:	Amanda's room					
Purpose:	Inform					
Audience:	Peers					
Item	**Sight**	**Taste**	**Touch**	**Smell**	**Hear**	**Emotion**
Walls	Rosy Pink					Favorite color
Ceiling	White					
Floors						
Dresser	Glossy white, neat, tidy		Smooth			
Photos	Black & white, color, family, friends					Love, acceptance
Bed	Four-Poster, white		Posts tall, molded, soft			Memories, quiet place, relaxing
Comforter	Roses, burgundy, deep green		Soft			Comforting
Stereo	Black				Classical music	Calming, soothing, refreshing
Closet	Mirrored doors, reflections		Cold glass			
Window	Woods		Lets in breeze			

Paragraph Process:

1. **Consider:**
   - *Topic*
   - *Purpose*
   - *Audience*
2. **Approach**
3. **Preliminary Topic Sentence**
4. **Supporting Information**
5. **Planning Outline**
6. **Formalize Topic Sentence**
7. **Rough Draft**
8. **Edit, Polish, Final Draft**

At this point, a topic sentence should be crafted and the items to support the contention selected for a Planning Outline. The supporting items must be arranged in a **logical sequence** such as left to right, top to bottom, internal to external. Next, it is time to write the first draft. The paragraph must then be reviewed to make sure the wording of each sentence is on topic and maintains the intended effect.

Descriptive wording may need to be improved and some items possibly eliminated. Even the topic sentence should be considered open for revision. Finally, a strong concluding sentence will end the paragraph.

In Illustrations 9B and 9C, the student will notice that the sample paragraph does not include every idea or description entered in the planner. This is because some ideas might not be pertinent to the topic. Also, relating an item to more than one sense may cause a paragraph to become wordy and tedious to read. Additionally, some of the information might not add to the effect of the paragraph. Only those items which best support the topic sentence and the writer's intended effect are selected and discussed.

Logical sequence is determined by the writer, but generally follows standard forms such as:

- Left to right
- Right to left
- Clockwise
- Counter-clockwise
- Top to bottom
- Bottom to top
- Least to greatest
- First to last
- Least interesting to most interesting
- Internal to external

9B - Descriptive Paragraph - Sample 1

Amanda's room is a place of peace and solitude. This calm starts with the walls and ceiling. Rosy pink walls bring a sense of comfort while the white paint on the ceiling gives the illusion of spaciousness. Her furnishings enhance this atmosphere. On top of a white, provincial dresser sit photos of family and friends. A four poster bed invites her to recline on its rose-covered bedspread while her radio emits her favorite classical music. Other surrounding features continue the tranquil setting. Reflections in the mirrored closet doors make the room seem spacious and cheerful. In that reflection, she can see woods outside her big window. This room is a hide-a-way where Amanda finds a peaceful retreat.

9C - Descriptive Paragraph - Sample 2 (Advanced Level)

The picturesque beauty of Multnomah Falls, located in Oregon's Columbia River Gorge, captivates its visitors. A striking background sets up for the stunning foreground. Vertical rock walls comprised of five layers of volcanic basalt line the gorge along the miles around the falls. Standing in contrast to these crumbling, brown walls of stone, leafy shrubs and trees soften the rock faces with deep green foliage. The manner in which the falls are tucked away into this background makes it even more arresting. Naturally, the falling water itself forms the most captivating part of the sight. Beautiful, spring-fed, white water plummets 620 feet from Larch Mountain to the rocks below the bridge where it calms in deep, dark pools. Falling away from the main stream of water are drops of watery mist which cascade onto the tourists below, offering a touch of refreshment on a hot summer's day. Adding to this beautiful scene is the eye-catching Benson Bridge, designed in classic style by Italian stone masons. Installed many years ago, its arched supports and horizontal lines contrast with the vertical water dropping behind it. What an engaging sight is this west coast landmark!

9.4 Literary Device

In this lesson, the student will implement the first of several literary devices, introduced on page 54, to be practiced in this course. **Figurative language** is the broad category under which the first few devices will fall. Figurative language compares two things that one would not generally think to compare. Thus, an author is said to be writing figuratively whenever he makes this kind of comparison.

Simile

The first figurative language technique is **simile**. A simile is the comparison of one concept or object with another in order to explain or clarify the first. This is done by use of the words "like" or "as." A simile works best when the comparison is made between subjects not normally associated. The following are examples of similes:

> *The peacock's calls, which filled the neighborhood, sounded just <u>like a woman's screams for help</u>.*
>
> *<u>Like a weather vane turning in the wind</u>, her mind changes with every opinion.*
>
> *<u>As the deer pants for the water</u>, so my soul longs after Thee.*
>
> *Endure hardship <u>as a strong soldier</u>.*

A simile is the comparison of one object with another using the words "like" or "as."

WEEK 9
Descriptive Paragraphs

Daily Assignments

———— **Day 1** ————

A. Reading Assignment:
Study the Week 9 lesson on descriptive paragraphs thoroughly.

B. Grammar Drill:
Drill the state of being verbs and helping verbs again today.

C. Sentence Drill:
Rewrite the following sentence placing the italicized word(s) in the most emphatic location.

> Josiah will need a *long* extension cord if he plans to set up the projector in the center of the room.

D. Lesson Exercise:
Answer the following questions in complete sentences.
1. What is the goal when writing a descriptive paragraph?
2. When writing descriptively, how may a writer better engage the reader?
3. What is a simile?

E. Writing Exercise:
1. *Brainstorm a descriptive paragraph on a topic approved by your instructor. Write your brainstorming list neatly, in a manner suitable for submission with your final draft.*

   > *Purpose: inform*
   > *Audience: instructor choice*
   > *Topic suggestion: scenic location*

2. *Write a topic sentence and create a planning outline for this descriptive paragraph. The planning outline will also be submitted to your instructor with your final draft.*

———— **Day 2** ————

A. Grammar Drill:
Continue reviewing the first four columns of prepositions.

B. Style Drill:
Identify the style point used in the following sentence.

> To assure company investors, a precise, thorough financial statement was issued.

C. Writing Exercise:
Draft the entire descriptive paragraph which you planned on day one. All drafts and final copies should be double spaced. This week's literary device, a simile, is to be included in the paragraph. It may be worked in any time between now and Day 4.

The number of sentences in your paragraph will depend on your academic level and expertise. See the introductory material on pages iii - iv for specific guidelines or ask your instructor.

Many students at this point find that their planning outline does not work or is not logical. If you find this to be so in your case, rework the outline or, if necessary, repeat the brainstorming process. Create a new copy of your topic sentence and planning outline.

Prepare a copy of your paragraph draft today, so that you can mark corrections on it tomorrow. This draft, with corrections, will be submitted to your instructor with your final draft on Day 5.

Day 3

A. Grammar Drill:
Continue to drill the prepositions you have studied thus far.

B. Formality Drill:
Using the formality and grammar rules explained in Lesson 2, rewrite the sentence below in proper form:

James felt like a fish out of water at the new campus.

C. Writing Exercise:
1. *Utilizing the Paragraph Checklist, begin to edit your paragraph draft from yesterday, marking corrections and changes on your rough draft. In addition, do the following:*

    a. *Think about where you can insert a simile.*

    b. *Add three different style points on this day.*

2. *Prepare a revised copy of your paragraph.*

Day 4

A. Grammar Drill:
Continue to drill the first four columns of prepositions.

B. Style Drill:
Identify the style point used in the following sentence.

Quietly and patiently spoke the woman.

C. Writing Exercise:

1. Go over your paragraph and correct all spelling, punctuation, and grammatical errors.

2. This week's literary device must be added to the paragraph by today. If you cannot fit the device into the assignment, write two sample sentences, each including this week's literary device, and submit them with your paragraph.

3. Make other improvements in words and phrases that may come to mind, according to the guidelines given on Day 3.

4. Prepare a revised draft of your paragraph.

Day 5

A. Grammar Drill:
Continue to rehearse the prepositions you have studied thus far.

B. Formality Drill:
Using the formality and grammar rules explained in Lesson 2, rewrite the sentence below in proper form:

They is going to the coast for a vacation.

C. Writing Exercise:

1. The final day to polish your paragraph has come. Read the paragraph aloud slowly and listen for problem areas. Now, have someone else read it to you; listen and be certain that the product is well-written.

2. Using the Paragraph Checklist, review your paragraph. Check off each guideline in the upper section when you have verified that you have followed it. In the lower section, mark the style points you have used. On your final draft, identify these style points by writing the corresponding number from the checklist directly above each one, and label the literary device.

3. Make certain that the assignment is double-spaced, has one-inch margins, has page numbering if needed, and that it includes the proper heading required by your instructor. These should include: Name, Date, Assignment, Purpose, Audience, Class, and Final Draft. See the next page for an illustration of proper heading and page formatting.

4. Submit your work to the instructor:
    a. Final draft paragraph
    b. Paragraph checklist
    c. Literary device, if created separately
    d. All drafts
    e. Topic sentence & planning outline
    f. Brainstorming

Sample Page Formatting and Numbering

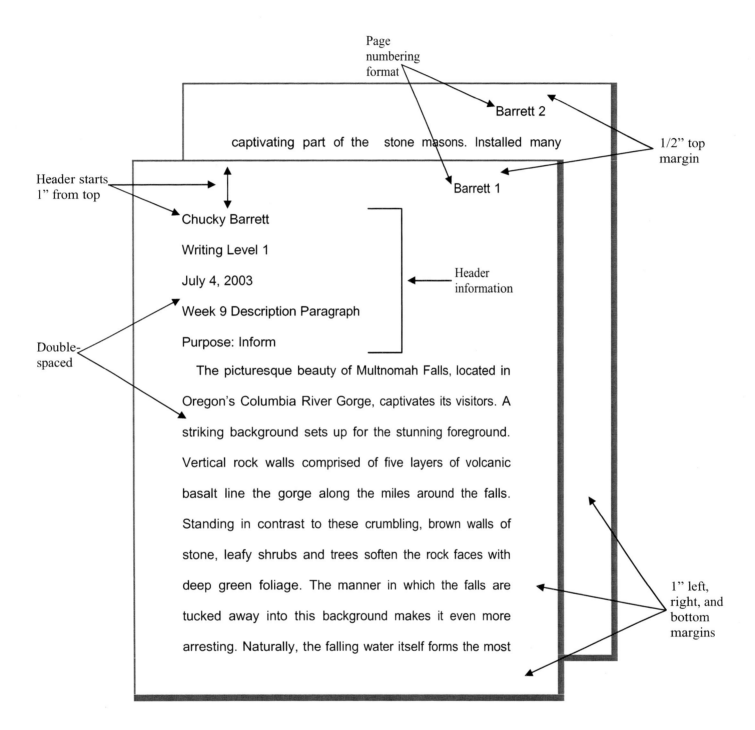

WEEK 10

Lesson: *Research, Documentation, and Ownership of Ideas*

10.1 Introduction

Why do research? A writer regularly needs to do research to gain general information on a subject or to expand the depth of the writing. Also, a writer can enhance his argument by citing material from reliable sources; however, any information a writer uses that is not his own must be properly documented and credited to the original author. This unit will discuss the research process, presentation of research material, and proper documentation of sources of supporting information.

10.2 Preliminary Research

If the writer does not know enough about a topic to take a position or decide on an approach, preliminary research will be necessary. One way to approach this research is to set up the potential topic as a question:

Do the Wright Brothers deserve to be inducted into the Aviation Hall of Fame?

To answer this question, general research of a wide variety of sources will be conducted. Information gathered may then prove to the writer that the answer should be "yes" or "no." At this point, the writer is ready to turn the question into a position statement, or contention, which he will set out to prove in the paragraph. The position statement becomes the basis for the paragraph's topic sentence:

The Wright Brothers deserve to be inducted into the Aviation Hall of Fame.

10.3 Researching Supporting Information

The next step, after forming a position statement, is to do further research of information to support the contention. A writer can draw supporting material from library materials, information spoken by experts on a topic, or reliable Internet material. Information must come from reliable sources. Content from junk mail, Internet chat rooms, discussion loops, or the like is not acceptable. Furthermore, some instructors may consider all Internet sources unreliable and not permissible for research papers.

10.4 Plagiarism

Ideas and words, whether written or spoken, actually belong to the originating author or speaker. Some students think that by simply restating an idea in their own words, it becomes their own. Rewording something, however, does not change ownership. Presenting someone else's ideas or words as if they are one's own is called **plagiarism**. In all forms of writing, plagiarism must be completely

Plagiarism is presenting someone else's ideas or words as if they are one's own.

Standard Bibliographic Information:
- authors' names
- editor's name
- date
- title
- publisher
- place of publication
- edition
- page numbers

avoided by giving credit to the source. If ever in doubt, the writer should document within his paragraph everything, whether words or ideas, gleaned from a source.

10.5 Recording Research

In order to document information or ideas he uses, a writer must record **standard bibliographic information** about each source researched. This would include: authors' names, date, title, publisher, place of publication, and edition (if any) written on a Working Bibliography page. In addition, an index card is used to record quotes, summaries, paraphrases, or ideas taken from a source along with page number or other reference. Each note is placed on a separate card. Below is a sample Bibliographic Information sheet and sample note cards. These should be carefully studied to learn their proper format.

10A - Example Research Records

Working Bibliography

1. Put That In Writing. Steve & Shari Barrett. 2002. Barrett's Bookshelf. Lake Oswego. Page 21.

2. "Housefly Life Cycle." Pritam Singh. (author) Internet. Available: <www.hortnet.co.nz/publications/hortfacts/hf401042.htm>. Accessed 10 June 2003.

3. "Housefly." Columbia Electronic Encyclopedia. 1994, 2000. Accessed 10 June 2003 <http://print.factmonster.com/ce6/sci/A0824306.html>.

Fly feeding habits   1

"The fly secretes digestive juices onto its food to liquefy it."

P. 21

Fly feeding habits   3

"They will gather round the lips, eyes and nursing bottles of very young children."

Internet - n. pag.

Working Bibliography: A rough draft listing of the bibliographic information for works that may be cited in the final paper.

Some instructors require that both bibliographic information and quotes be recorded on index cards. Others do not require note cards and allow the student to establish his or her own system. No matter what method is used, careful records must be kept of each source and any corresponding ideas, facts, quotations, paraphrases, or summaries.

10.6 Presentation of research

Generally when researching, the writer will gather more information than is practical to use. Therefore, the number of sources and useable material will need to be narrowed down to what is most appropriate for the given assignment. Next, a decision must be made regarding how to present it. The selected research material can be presented in four ways:

    A. **Quotation** is the most straight forward way to present research material. If a writer is going to use <u>any</u> of a source author's own wording, it is best to quote so that there is no chance of misrepresenting the material as being the writer's own. Quotations must be exactly as stated by the source and must be credited to the author or speaker.

    B. **Summary** is a technique in which just the main points of a source, author or speaker, are condensed and stated in the writer's own words. A summary is to be very short and is not to include any opinion about the points cited. Even though the wording is the writer's own, the source must be credited.

    C. **Paraphrasing** is the restatement of a source's words in the writer's own words. It differs from summary in that a paraphrase is not limited to just the main points and may, in fact, be longer than the original source. Again, proper credit must be given to the original source.

    D. **Use of an idea** requires documentation as well. An opinion or perspective drawn from another's work and pursued in one's own work is information that must be given proper credit. In such an instance, the source would be cited at a natural break in the essay, generally at the end of a paragraph. If the paragraph contains more than one idea from different sources, the ideas are documented in the order they are presented.

Formality flaws within quotes are not to be corrected.

10.7 Treatment of Quotes

Quotes are presented differently in the paragraph, depending on length. Quotations up to four lines long need no special treatment and may remain within the normal written text enclosed in quotation marks. These are referred to as **"integrated quotes."** Quotations more than four lines long should appear as a separate block of text, indented one inch from the left margin, double-spaced, without quotation marks. This is called a **"block quote."** The sentence of text before the block quote will usually end with a colon.

Integrated quotes remain within the normal written text, enclosed in quotation marks.

10.8 Proper Summary or Paraphrase

When presenting material as summary or paraphrase, the writer does not have the privilege of using the exact wording of an original source. Nevertheless, one will occasionally notice a quoted phrase within summarized source material. It should be understood that this is proper to do *only* when conveyance of a precise point or meaning is necessary. Such use of exact source wording, however, must

Block quotes appear as a separate block of text indented one inch from the left margin without quotation marks.

be minimal and always enclosed in quotation marks.

Illustration 10B below shows the right and wrong ways to summarize or paraphrase source information. In both incorrect samples, the plagiarized phrases are underlined to show how to avoid copying words that belong to others.

10B - Summary and Paraphrase Examples

Original Text:	No growing boy can afford to stop eating for a week, or a day; and no youth, ambitious to grow intellectually, can afford to let a day go by without a little solid reading. The task need not be long: twenty minutes' physical exercise will keep up the muscles, once they have been developed, and a half hour's keen intellectual work will keep up one's culture, providing the youth is alert and awake all day long, looking out upon life with hungry eyes, and harvesting truth on every side. A notebook and lead pencil will make a record of a score of great facts, picked up by the youth who has open vision and an observing mind. — Newell Dwight Hillis, "The Contagion of Character" (Thurber 45). Thurber, Samuel. Editor. *Precis Writing for American Schools*. Boston: Little, Brown, and Company, 1927.
Plagiarized Summary:	Just as short exercise is sufficient to keep up the muscles, so a half hour's keen work of stimulating reading will keep the intellect sharp. Recording one's observations with notebook and pencil will also be of benefit.
Proper Summary: (Must be documented)	Just as a short twenty minutes of exercise per day will maintain a fit body, so thirty minutes of stimulating reading every day is sufficient to maintain a growing intellect. Recording what is learned can be of additional benefit.
Plagiarized Paraphrase:	No growing young man can afford to go without food for a week, or a day; and no young person who desires to grow intellectually, should skip any day without a little reading. It does not take long; only twenty minutes physical exercise will keep a person in shape, and thirty minutes of intellectual activity by the young person who is alert and looking at life with hungry eyes, will keep up one's learning. Great information picked up by the youth with vision will be recorded with a notebook and lead pencil.
Proper Paraphrase: (Must be documented)	A maturing young man cannot risk going without food for long, or even short periods of time. In the same way no young person who desires to develop intellectually, can risk even one day without spending time in a book. Once one is in shape, physical conditioning can be maintained with a mere twenty minutes of exercise a day. The time required to maintain the intellect is also short for attentive youth who search passionately for truth in every quarter. Maintaining a written record can only add to the lessons learned by the perceptive, attentive young person.

10.9 MLA Documentation

MLA website: www.mla.org

The Modern Language Association (MLA) publishes a style manual, setting forth guidelines for documenting sources in writing assignments in the humanities - English, literature, art, history, and philosophy. This method of documentation is referred to as MLA Style and includes these basic parts: an in-text citation, and a page or pages listing bibliographic information about the sources. For a complete explanation on citing sources, refer to the most recent version of the *MLA Handbook for Writers of Research Papers*. This section is designed to present the student with sufficient information to understand the basics of documenting sources.

A. In-Text Reference (Citation)

Source information must first be documented within the text. The guiding principle for this citation is that it must include sufficient information to equip the reader to locate the source on the "Works Cited" page which is described below. Generally, the information in a parenthetical reference includes the name of the author, the page number from which the research was taken, and at times, all or part of the title of the work. This in-text documentation may be done in one of two ways.

(1) Parenthetical Reference

The first, and most common, way to cite sources is with a **parenthetical reference** placed within the written text after a quotation, or other use of source material. This parenthetical citation must include the first word, or words, from the listing of the source on the "Works Cited" page. For instance, the documentation may look like: (Barrett 21). This in-text citation tells the reader that the source of the information was a work written by someone with the last name "Barrett," and that it came from page 21.

Some exceptions to the standard format do occur. For instance, care must be taken to use the correct form when citing multiple sources by the same author. In these cases the author's name and a word, or words, from the title to distinguish the work must be cited along with the page number:

Reference 1, Source 1: (Barrett, *Writing* 21)
Reference 1, Source 2: (Barrett, *Coping* 45)

(2) Integrated Reference

The second method involves integrating all or part of the information into the flow of the written text. For example, one may name the author or perhaps even the title and page number within the written text. If all the required citation elements are included in the text, no additional citation is needed. Any reference information not written within the text must appear in parentheses following the source material.

Finally, parenthetical citations will differ depending on the type of source. In some special instances, textual citation may require different or additional components. Also, some sources are best referenced directly in the written text. For common variations of parenthetical citations and their uses, refer to Appendix D on page 202-205.

A parenthetical reference is made up of parenthesis placed around identifying words which direct the reader to the source listing on the "Works Cited" page.

While MLA documentation and formatting is taught in this course, Chicago Style is the proper method for textbooks. Therefore, the student should not be confused when parts of this text do not follow MLA guidelines.

B. Ending Punctuation with Parenthetical References

When including parenthetical citations at the end of sentences, punctuation varies as illustrated by the partial sentence samples below:

	Quotation:	Summary/Paraphrase
Statement:	"...each day" (Barrett 94). Barrett details how "... each day" (94).	... daily (Barrett 94).
Question:	"... each day?" (Barrett 94).	... daily? (Barrett 94).
Exclamation:	"... each day!" (Barrett 94).	...amounts daily! (Barrett 94).

C. "Works Cited" Page

The second component of MLA documentation involves an alphabetical listing of all cited sources at the end of the essay, generally on a separate page entitled "Works Cited." Information for this page is to be drawn from the Working Bibliography page created during research. This title should be centered at the top of the page; the first listing starts two lines down from the title. The first line of each work listed is not indented; however, if the citation extends to more than one line, the additional lines are indented. Sources listed on this page should appear in alphabetical order. Appendix D gives formats for listing various sources on the "Works Cited" page.

"Works Cited" Page Format:
1. *Title centered*
2. *First entry two lines down*
3. *First line of entry not indented*
4. *Additional lines indented*
5. *Double space between sources*
6. *Sources listed in alphabetical order*
7. *Proper order of bibliographic information based on Appendix D*

10C - Sample Works Cited Page Layout

Works Cited

Barrett, S. R. *Coping With Your Problem Pet.* Portland: Sisterly Love Publishing, 2002.

Myers, L. *Supporting Owners of Problem Pets.* Nampa: Hilltop Publishing, 2002.

Tish, N. *Finding a Home for the Unwanted Pet.* Caldwell: Kindhearted Publications, 1991.

D. "Works Consulted" Page

Some instructors may also require the student to document all sources which were consulted during research on a page entitled "Works Consulted." The listing of works follows the same format as a "Works Cited" page. Sometimes the student will submit only a "Works Consulted" page. In other instances, both a "Works Cited" page and a "Works Consulted" page may be required when the number of sources cited within the paper is less than the references researched. If only a "Works Consulted" page is required, the student will still be able to identify sources referenced in the writing by way of the parenthetical in-text citation.

WEEK 10
Research, Documentation, and Ownership of Ideas

Daily Assignments

——————— **Day 1** ———————

A. Reading Assignment:
Read the complete Week 10 Lesson, taking time to review all the MLA documentation formats. Be certain that you understand how to properly cite a source without plagiarism.

B. Lesson Exercise:
Answer the following questions in complete sentences.
1. Before choosing a perspective or approach on a topic, what might be needed?
2. What are the components of standard bibliographic information?
3. In what four ways may a writer present research information?
4. What is a parenthetical reference?

C. Writing Exercise:
You are going to practice gathering research information for a potential paragraph or essay on the solar system.
1. Begin by looking up information on the solar system in a traditional encyclopedia (not on the Internet). Copy two **quotes** on the characteristics of different planets and two **quotes** on the characteristics of meteors onto note cards. Each quote should be placed on a separate card. Format each note card as instructed in the lesson.
2. Write the proper information on a Working Bibliography page as source 1 (see page 72)
3. Find two more quotes about planets and two more quotes about meteors from at least one other book (not an encyclopedia). Copy these quotes, as well, onto note cards in proper format.
4. Write the appropriate information for citing each book onto your Working Bibliography page, continuing to number each source as you study it.

——————— **Day 2** ———————

A. Grammar Drill:
If possible, record yourself reading the entire preposition list onto a tape. Listen to the list several times today.

B. Style Drill:
Identify the style point used in the following sentence.

After his wife's younger sister died at a young age, Charles Dickens created his character, Little Nell.

C. Writing Exercise:
You are going to practice gathering research information for a potential paragraph or essay on Samuel Clemens.

1. Begin by looking up information on Samuel Clemens (Mark Twain) in a traditional encyclopedia (not on the Internet). Copy two **quotes** about some of the difficulties he faced in his life, and two **quotes** about one or two of the books he wrote onto note cards. Each quote should be placed on a separate card. Format each note card as instructed in the lesson.
2. Write the proper information on a Working Bibliography page as source 1.
3. Find two more quotes about Samuel Clemens's life and two more quotes about the same book(s) from at least one other source (not an encyclopedia). Copy these quotes, as well, onto note cards in proper format.
4. Write the appropriate information for citing each book onto your Working Bibliography page, continuing to number each source as you study it.

Day 3

A. Grammar Drill:
Listen again to the prepositions on tape several times today.

B. Formality Drill:
Using the formality and grammar rules explained in Lesson 2, rewrite the sentence below in proper form:

When one goes to the store, they most certainly should have some means to pay for any purchases.

C. Writing Exercise:
You are going to practice gathering research information for a potential paragraph or essay on George Washington Carver.

1. Begin by looking up information on George Washington Carver in a traditional encyclopedia (not on the Internet). Copy two **quotes** about his background, and two **quotes** about his innovations with agricultural products onto note cards. Each quote should be placed on a separate card. Format each note card as instructed in the lesson.
2. Write the proper information on a Working Bibliography page as source 1.
3. Find two more quotes about George Washington Carver's life and two more quotes about his innovative ideas from at least one other source (not an encyclopedia). Copy these quotes, as well, onto note cards in proper format.

4. Write the appropriate information for citing each book onto your Working Bibliography page, continuing to number each source as you study it.

—————— Day 4 ——————

A. Grammar Drill:
Listen again to the prepositions on tape three different times today.

B. Style Drill:
Identify the style point used in the following sentence.

For the families of the Apollo 13 astronauts, the succeeding days were very stressful.

C. Writing Exercise:
You are going to practice creating parenthetical references and a Works Cited Page.

1. *On a sheet of paper, copy each quotation below. Then, using the page number and bibliographic information given, add a proper parenthetical reference according to the guidelines in Lesson 10 and Appendix D.*

    a. **Quote from book by one author**: "Aerobic exercise of any kind has the power to calm jangled nerves and improve bad moods. And when it's done every day, it can enhance self-esteem and combat depression." Page 35

    <u>Bibliographic Information</u>: *Prevention's Complete Book of Walking.* Maggie Spilner. Published by Rodale Inc. 2000

    b. **Quote from book by two authors**: "By contrast, exercise increases the body's metabolism, and this effect persists for as long as 6 to 24 hours after exercising moderately for only 30 minutes." Page 241

    <u>Bibliographic Information</u>: *Healthy Runner's Handbook.* By Lyle J. Micheli, M.D. & Mark Jenkins. Published by Human Kinetics. Champaign, Illinois. 1996

    c. **Quote from book by one author**: "What is walking good for? Here's the quick answer: your heart, lungs, blood, muscles, bones and joints, brain, gastrointestinal tract, immune system, perhaps even eyes and ears, and most definitely mood and spirit." Page 12

    <u>Bibliographic Information</u>: *The Complete Guide to Walking.* By Mark Fenton. Published by Lyons Press. New York. 2001

2. *On a separate sheet of paper, write a proper "Works Cited" page for the above sources. Follow the format shown in Illustration 10C, page 76.*

Day 5

A. Grammar Drill:
Listen again to the prepositions on tape several times today.

B. Formality Drill:
Using the formality and grammar rules explained in Lesson 2, rewrite the sentence below in proper form:

When they realized that Apollo 13 was damaged and might not get back to earth, the NASA engineers started sweating bullets.

C. Style Drill:
Identify the style point used in the following sentence.

Struggling to repair their ailing spacecraft were the Apollo 13 astronauts.

D. Writing Exercise:
You are going to practice creating parenthetical references and a Works Cited Page.

1. *On a sheet of paper, copy each quotation below. Then, using the page number and bibliographic information given, add a proper parenthetical reference according to the guidelines in Lesson 10 and Appendix D.*

    a. **Quote from book by one author**: "As you document your own paper you need to keep two main purposes in mind: first, you must let your readers know where you found your material, and second, you must make it possible for them to locate and use that material if they wish." Page 203

    <u>Bibliographic Information</u>: *Successful Writing.* 2nd ed. Maxine C. Hairston. 1981, 1986. New York. Published by W.W. Norton & Company.

    b. **Quote from book by one author:** "Accuracy with documentation signals to the reader that you have both researched the subject and given proper credit to other scholars, rather than plagiarized the sources by borrowing without acknowledgment." Page 133

    <u>Bibliographic Information</u>: *Writing Research Papers.* 6th ed. James D. Lester. 1990. Published by Scott, Foresman/Little, Brown. Glenview, Illinois.

    c. **Quote from book by two authors:** "Unlike the robber, however, some plagiarists fail to realize what they have done wrong. Students who once copied encyclopedia articles to satisfy school assignments may never have learned the necessity of using quotation marks and citing sources. Others may think that by paraphrasing a quotation or summarizing an idea — that is, by putting it into their own words — they have turned it into public property." Page 459

    <u>Bibliographic Information</u>: *The Borzoi Handbook for Writers.* 2nd ed. Frederick Crews & Sandra Schor. New York. Published by Alfred A. Knopf. 1989.

2. *On a separate sheet of paper, write a proper "Works Cited" page for the above sources. Follow the format shown in Illustration 10C, page 76.*

WEEK 11

Lesson: *Definition Paragraphs*

11.1 Introduction

The **definition paragraph** is unique from other paragraphs in that it is generally included in a larger essay to explain a word or an idea so the reader can understand the point of view or analysis that follows. Simply put, this paragraph expounds on a term or concept in such a way that the meaning is clear to the reader. For purposes of this lesson, the definition paragraph will be developed as a single unit, and its goal will be to use words to give the reader a clear picture, or understanding of a term or idea.

A definition paragraph makes a term understandable to the reader.

11.2 Topic Sentence

Topic sentences for definition paragraphs can be challenging, so it is critical to read this section carefully. Since the purpose of this paragraph will almost invariably be to inform the reader, a topic sentence will offer a fairly simple position. For example,

The word "play" can have a dual meaning.

It would not be appropriate for the topic sentence to state the definition. Rather, the writer should set the stage for presenting the definition.

11.3 Treatment of Word Being Defined

Special guidelines should be followed for presenting the word being defined in this type of paragraph. Since the word being defined is not used in its standard function in the sentences and paragraph, the word is to be enclosed in quotation marks as done in the sample topic sentence above as well as in the sample paragraph at the end of this lesson. Placing the word in quotes shows the reader that the word is separated from its normal usage.

11.4 Paragraph Content

Content of this type of paragraph will vary, but every point included should serve to make the term understandable to the reader. The proper starting place for content would likely be the definition, either quoted or paraphrased from a dictionary or other authoritative source. Additional items which may be considered for use include: synonyms, grammatical function, descriptive phrasing, **etymology**, example, comparison, **analysis**, or **synthesis**. Obviously, only some of this extensive list will comprise the paragraph, and every item chosen should serve a strong purpose. This is not a paragraph which is just filled with a list of ideas. Since stand alone paragraphs will be written for this lesson, defining words which have broad application works best.

Etymology explains the origin or history of a word.

Analysis is the separation of something into parts to determine the important points.

Synthesis is the combination of parts into a whole.

The objective with this paragraph is to give the reader a precise understanding of the term. Therefore, along with strong content, one must use precise words in this type of paragraph. Words, such as "huge" or "many," which convey only general meanings should be avoided. Again, the goal of a definition paragraph must be to impart exact information. Illustrations 11A and 11B on page 83 demonstrate the development of a definition paragraph and should be studied.

11.5 Concluding Sentence

Frequently, students forget to include a proper concluding sentence when writing a definition paragraph. Nonetheless, this basic component is necessary to summarize content and point the reader back to the main contention.

11.6 Literary Device

Parallelism is putting similar ideas into repeated grammatical construction for emphasis or clarity, often in the same sentence. This can appear as a repetition of words or phrases, or it can be parallel grammatical structure. For instance,

Parallel verb patterns:
Olivia went running, jumping, and skipping down the hill.

Ashley could not have seen and could not have known the outcome of her wise decision.

Parallel phrases:
She gladly received the awards for her son, for her daughter, and for her husband.

The family decided to go to the store, to purchase the stereo, and to set it up in the living room.

Singing on her way, she traveled down the road. Skipping by any dangers, she moved past the house. Smiling at her neighbors, she greeted each one.

> *Parallelism is the repetition of structure for emphasis or clarity.*

The Gettysburg Address offers several more examples of parallelism, some of which are marked in the text below:

> Four score and seven years ago, our fathers brought forth upon this continent a new nation: <u>conceived</u> in liberty, and <u>dedicated</u> to the proposition that all men are created equal. Now we are engaged in a great civil war. . .testing whether that nation, or any nation <u>so conceived</u> and <u>so dedicated</u>. . . can long endure. We are met on a great battlefield of that war. We have come to dedicate a portion of that field as a final resting place for those who here gave their lives that that nation might live. It is altogether fitting and proper that we should do this. But, in a larger sense, <u>we cannot dedicate</u>. . .<u>we cannot consecrate</u>. . . <u>we cannot hallow</u> this ground. The brave men, living and dead, who struggled here have consecrated it, far above our poor power to add or detract. The world will little note, nor long remember, what we say here, but it can never forget what they did here. <u>It is for us</u> the living, rather, to be dedicated here to the unfinished work which they who fought here have thus far so nobly advanced. <u>It is rather for us</u> to be here dedicated to the great task remaining before us. . .<u>that</u> from these honored dead we take increased devotion to that cause for which they gave the last full measure of devotion. . . <u>that</u> we here highly resolve that these dead shall not have died in vain. . . <u>that</u> this nation, under God, shall have a new birth of freedom. . . and that government <u>of the people</u>. . .<u>by the people</u>. . .<u>for the people</u>. . . shall not perish from the earth.
>
> Lincoln's **Gettysburg Address**, given November 19, 1863 on the battlefield near Gettysburg, Pennsylvania, USA

11A - Planning Outline for Definition Paragraph on "Humility"

Topic sentence: Understanding the meaning of "humility" helps one see that this trait should be practiced.

1. Define and explain
   A. Definition
   B. Explanation

2. Should humility be practiced?
   A. Jonathan Edwards
   B. King Solomon

3. Example of humble people
   A. George Washington
   B. Jeff Dachis

Concluding sentence: One can see from these brief examples that humility should be embraced.

11B - Sample Definition Paragraph on the Word "Humility"

Understanding the meaning of "humility" helps one see that this trait should be practiced. Perhaps the simple definition is the best place to grasp this attribute's significance. By definition, humility means a lack of pride, arrogance, and self-dependence (American). The meaning indicates that a truly humble person, while he possesses unique giftings, is not conceited, prideful, and does not consider himself more important than he ought. Should everyone practice humility? Jonathan Edwards, an Eighteenth century minister, said, "Humility is a most essential and distinguishing trait in all true piety." King Solomon wrote in Proverbs 29:23, "A man's pride will bring him low, but a humble spirit will obtain honor" (NASB). Distinguished and talented people have applied humility to their lives. George Washington, a man known for his humility, demonstrated its long reaching impact. His chosen title, "Mr. President," for the office which he held, reflected the humility in his life. Interestingly, that mark of Washington's humility continues today as Americans still refer to the president of their country by this unassuming title. In recent years, one company chief executive officer has also adopted this valuable attribute. Jeff Dachis, who started the flourishing "Razorfish" Internet consulting business, was known for his cocky arrogance. Then the man received his comeuppance when the company fell on hard times. In order to save the business, he made humbling financial sacrifices and corrected his attitude. Now a changed person, Dachis is quoted as saying, "Be humble because in success, humility will win, and in failure, humility will win" (Green). One can see from these brief examples that every person would do well to embrace a modest estimate of his own worth.

Works Cited

Edwards, Jonathan. "Humility." Internet. Available: www.eternalifeministries.cor/ humility.htm. September 15, 2002.

Green, Heather. "A Web Hotshot Learns Humility." *Business Week Online.* Internet. Available: www.businessweek.com:/print/magazine/content/01_12/ b3724635.htm?mainwindow. September 15, 2002.

"Humility." *American Dictionary of the English Language.* San Francisco: F.A.C.E., 1967.

New American Standard Bible. The Lockman Foundation. Nashville: Thomas Nelson, 1978.

WEEK 11
Definition Paragraphs

Daily Assignments

Day 1

A. Reading Assignment:
Study the Week 11 lesson on definition paragraphs thoroughly.

B. Lesson Exercise:
1. Answer the following questions in complete sentences.

   a. What is the purpose of the definition paragraph?
   b. What is parallelism?

2. Correct the following examples of faulty parallel structure.

   a. The young boy went <u>running</u>, <u>jumping</u>, and he fell past the onlookers.
   b. Their ambitious neighbor was <u>landscaping</u> the yard, he <u>dug</u> the pond, and the fountain was <u>installed</u> in time for the special event.
   c. <u>No one can</u> truly know, <u>no one can</u> truly appreciate, and <u>nobody will</u> ever value this project for the immense labor that went into it.

C. Writing Exercise:
1. Brainstorm a definition paragraph on a topic approved by your instructor. Print your brainstorming list neatly, in a manner suitable for submission with your final draft.
   Purpose: inform
   Audience: instructor choice
   Topic suggestions: a character trait, an interesting verb

2. Do research for supporting information. Gather bibliographic information, general notes on the topic, and prepare quotations, summaries, or paraphrases to offer in support of your position as described in the Week 10 Lesson. You will need to cite two different sources in the paragraph and create a "Works Cited" page.

3. Write a topic sentence and create a planning outline for this definition paragraph. The planning outline will also be submitted to your instructor with your final draft.

Day 2

A. Grammar Drill:
Continue rehearsing all the prepositions from memory.

B. Style Drill:
Identify the style point used in the following sentence.

   For his family's vacation to Canada, Lloyd quickly built a camper.

C. Writing Exercise:
Draft the entire definition paragraph which you planned on Day 1. This draft should be double-spaced. Insert proper citations for any research evidence included. This week's literary device, parallelism, is to be included in the paragraph. It may be added any time between now and Day 4.

Again, the number of sentences in your paragraph will depend on your academic level and instructor's choice.

If your planning outline does not work or is not logical, re-work the outline or, if necessary, repeat the brainstorming process. Create a new copy of your topic sentence and planning outline.

Create a copy of your paragraph draft today so that you can mark corrections on it tomorrow. This draft, with corrections, will be submitted to your instructor with your final draft on Day 5.

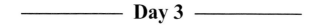

Day 3

A. Grammar Drill:
Continue drilling all the prepositions today.

B. Formality Drill:
Using the formality and grammar rules explained in Lesson 2, rewrite the sentence below in proper form:

Madame Defarge, another of Dickens' characters, wouldn't stop knitting as she sat in the wine shop watching for spies.

C. Writing Exercise:
1. *Now, begin to edit your paragraph draft from yesterday, marking corrections and changes on your rough draft. Stick with the following guidelines:*

   a. *For this definition paragraph, work at citing examples and explanations which might be of particular interest to your audience.*
   b. *Think about where you can insert parallelism.*
   c. *Try to vary sentence structure: simple, compound, complex, compound-complex.*
   d. *Be certain that you use transitions to make the ideas flow together.*
   e. *Add three different style points on this day.*
   f. *Place important ideas at points of emphasis within sentences.*

2. *Prepare a revised copy of your paragraph, hand-written or computer printed.*

Day 4

A. Grammar Drill:
Again, drill the entire preposition list.

B. Style Drill:
Identify the style point used in the following sentence.

When the sergeant gave the order, the soldier fell into step with the rest of the platoon.

C. Writing Exercise:
1. *Go over your paragraph and correct all spelling, punctuation, and grammatical errors.*
2. *This week's literary device must be added to the paragraph by this day. If you cannot fit the device into the assignment, write two sample sentences, each including this week's literary device, and submit them with your paragraph.*
3. *Make other improvements in words and phrases that may come to mind according to the guidelines given on Day 3.*
4. *Prepare a revised draft of your paragraph.*

──────── Day 5 ────────

A. Grammar Drill:
Continue to drill the complete prepositions list.

B. Formality Drill:
Using the formality and grammar rules explained in Lesson 2, rewrite the sentence below in proper form:

In order for the neighbor to work on his fountain, they needed to drive equipment across the Barretts' property.

C. Writing Exercise:
1. *The final day to polish your paragraph has come. Read the paragraph aloud slowly and listen for problem areas. Now, have someone else read it to you so that you can listen and be certain that the product is well-written.*
2. *Using the Paragraph Checklist, review your paragraph. Check off each guideline in the upper section when you have verified that you have followed it. In the lower section, mark the style points you have used. On your final draft, identify these style points by writing the corresponding number from the checklist directly above each one, and label the literary device.*
3. *Make certain that the assignment is double-spaced, has one inch margins, has page numbering if needed, and that it includes the proper heading required by your instructor (see page 69).*
4. *Submit your work to the instructor:*
   a. *Final draft paragraph*
   b. *Works Cited page, as applicable*
   c. *Literary device, if created separately*
   d. *Paragraph checklist*
   e. *All drafts*
   f. *Topic sentence & planning outline*
   g. *Brainstorming*

WEEK 12

Lesson: *Thinking Like a Teacher*

12.1 Introduction

Understanding the expectations of an instructor or a supervisor is a critical skill. Although expectations will differ with the person, some basic components should be present in any paragraph or essay which fits standard form. Also, instructors frequently hold to standard thought patterns as they evaluate written work. Therefore, in this lesson, the student will become familiar with the General Grading Form which is located in Appendix E on page 206. Spending time learning these thought patterns will ultimately benefit the student by equipping him to better evaluate his own work.

Each component of the grading form is listed below followed by questions an instructor might ask when evaluating an assignment. The student should spend some time reviewing the grading form and becoming familiar with the questions associated with each component.

12.2 Grading Form Components

A. Organization and Content

(1) *Topic sentence*
- Does this topic sentence state the exact purpose of the paragraph?
- Does it state the purpose in an interesting manner which engages the reader?
- Is there any way in which this topic sentence should or could set the tone for the paragraph?

(2) *Supporting information*
- Does all the supporting information pertain exactly to the topic stated?
- If the content veers off topic, how much of it is topical?
- Is the information unified in that it works as a cohesive whole to prove the topic sentence?

(3) *Good use of facts or examples*
- If the right information is included, is it presented in a manner which supports the topic sentence?
- Is there enough information or evidence?

(4) *Logical arrangement*
- Has the writer presented the material so that it flows logically?
- Does the progression of points work to convince the reader?

(5) *Final sentence*
- Does this sentence restate the contention or sum up the content of the paragraph using new and interesting words?

In this instance, the term, "leap of logic" refers to presenting of supporting material in a disconnected manner or without continuity.

B. **Impression**

(1) Concise
- Does the writer use frivolous and unnecessary words?

(2) Includes necessary and complete explanation
- Is the topic and contention fully explained so that the reader truly understands what is being said?
- Are there **"leaps of logic"** or unsupported contentions?

(3) Command of vocabulary
- Does the student wield a large enough vocabulary that he is equipped to explain himself clearly?
- Are words used accurately according to their defined meanings?
- Does the student use a variety of vocabulary, or does he repeat a term or terms over and over?

(4) Uses strong verbs, descriptive adjectives and adverbs
- How many state of being verbs does the writer use?
- Are descriptive adjectives and adverbs added which give the reader a more vivid mental picture?

(5) Specific wording
- Does the student avoid general terms when he could use more specific ones?
- Does the student use words such as "stuff," "things," "a lot," "a bunch"?

(6) Flows well
- Does the student effectively use transition words, phrases, and sentences?
- Are there run-on sentences?
- Does the paper bog down by focusing too much on one point and failing to move on to others?

(7) Proper emphasis
- Has the student focused on the proper ideas?
- Has the student placed emphatic ideas at the first or end of sentences?

(8) Fulfills purpose, targets audience
- Does the paragraph inform or persuade as intended?
- Is there any doubt about the target audience?

(9) Variety of sentence lengths and types
- How many of each structural type (simple, compound, complex, compound-complex) of sentences has the student used?
- Are there any fragments or run-on sentences?

C. Mechanical Errors
- How many words are spelled incorrectly?
- Are necessary capital letters included?
- Are punctuation marks used appropriately and when needed?
- Are there grammar errors in the paper?
- Does the writer write with appropriate formality for the setting?

D. Other Requirements

(1) Documentation
- Has the student included documentation: in text, "Works Cited" page?
- Is there material which has not been documented which should have been?
- Is all documentation formatted properly?

(2) Literary Device
- Did the student use the appropriate required literary device in this assignment? Is it marked so the teacher can readily identify it?

(3) Style points
- Has the student used the assigned number of required style points, and have they been marked for the instructor?

(4) Checklist
- Has the student included a checklist? Is the upper section properly filled out?
- If any items on the list are not applicable, has the student indicated this, or has he simply gone down the list checking points with disregard?
- Has the student marked the style points used?

(5) Outline, Drafts, Brainstorming
- Has the student included a planning outline?
- Has the student created early drafts and made genuine efforts to improve the assignment?
- Has student included brainstorming work?

(6) Presentation
- Is the final draft properly formatted for presentation to the instructor? Margins? Font size and style? Page numbering?
- Is the proper heading included on the paper?
- Are items together in the proper order?

12.3 Scoring

Evaluating written work can be very challenging. Most components in the grading form involve subjective evaluation; in other words, personal opinion. For example, whether or not a paragraph has a topic sentence is **objective**, but whether it is engaging is **subjective**. What pleases one reader may not please another.

Objective refers to a goal or aim which is real and identifiable by everyone, regardless of individual opinion. Facts are objective.

Subjective refers to ideas or opinions which are held in the mind of each individual. These opinions will differ from person to person; thus, opinions are subjective.

How does one determine an actual score? The recommended method is to assume full points for each component; then deduct points for lack of quality based on the questions given above. Deductions may be in half points. Obviously, if a component, such as the concluding sentence, is missing entirely, the points will be zero. Otherwise, each component on the grading form should receive some points. Full points should be reserved for superior work; average work should receive about seventy-five percent of the available points.

Learning to judge the points to award is a matter of experience. For this reason, the student will spend this week evaluating sample paragraphs with the grading form and discussing his evaluations with the teacher. The goal is for the student to learn to recognize quality work as well as common faults and, thereby, to better evaluate his own work.

12.4 Conclusion

A primary focus of this course, from this point forward, is evaluation and editing of one's own writing. When preparing a paragraph checklist for an assignment, or when editing an assignment, the student should routinely review the ideas in this chapter, examining whether his or her writing fulfills the grading form requirements.

WEEK 12
Thinking Like a Teacher

Daily Assignments

———— **Day 1** ————

A. Reading Assignment:
Study the Week 12 lesson on thinking like a teacher.

B. Lesson Exercise:

1. *Based on the guidelines given in this week's lesson, critique the following paragraph, marking scores, comments, and corrections on a grading form copied from Appendix E.*

   Assignment: describe Thanksgiving dinner
   Type of paragraph: descriptive paragraph
   Purpose: inform or persuade
   Audience: someone who was not at the Thanksgiving dinner

   Thanksgiving is a national holiday, which comes once a year, when friends and family come together to share a delicious meal. The main dish is the roasted turkey. Its dark meat is course, and the light meat is tender. Tasty, cornbread stuffing accompanies the turkey. A light, brown gravy and fluffy, white, mashed potatoes accompanies the main course. However, the gravy served this year was too salty for the taste buds of the diners. Maroon-colored, jellied cranberries jiggled on a bed of crisp lettuce as it was past. Diners could hardly wait to sample its tart flavor alongside the salty gravy. Fresh dinner rolls were slathered with butter and jelly by the delighted diners. Steamed vegetables of broccoli and cauliflower added some color, while the tossed and fruit salads added more splashes of color to the meal. There is pumpkin pie, cinnamon rolls, apple pie, and homemade ice cream for dessert. What a delicious meal the Smith family shares together each year!

2. *Discuss your evaluation with your instructor. Instructor should see answer key for full explanation.*

———— **Day 2** ————

A. Grammar Drill:
Continue reviewing the prepositions.

B. Style Drill:
Identify the style point used in the following sentence.

   Because he so impacted the planning and acceptance of the Constitution, James Madison has become known as the "father" of the Constitution.

C. **Lesson Exercise:**
1. *Based on the guidelines given in this week's lesson, critique the following paragraph, marking scores, comments, and corrections on a grading form copied from Appendix E.*

   Assignment: describe Thanksgiving dinner
   Type of paragraph: descriptive paragraph
   Purpose: inform or persuade
   Audience: someone who was not at the Thanksgiving dinner

   Thanksgiving dinner was filled with delicious foods. Family members, arriving at Grandma's house, were met with a beautifully decorated home. As extended family arrived, the holiday spirit was everywhere. Relatives, who had not seen one another all year, embraced warmly. Fragrances of sizzling turkey filled the home. When it came time to eat, everyone loved the traditional delicacies. In the center of the table, rested the perfectly roasted turkey. Its golden color enticed all to sample its meat. In addition, bread crumbs and yummy vegetables made up the stuffing which was inside the turkey. The traditional cranberry sauce jiggled slightly in the dish as everyone scooted close to the table. Steaming hot mashed potatoes smothered in gravy seemed to dissolve instantly when they hit the tongue. Sticky, sweet yams and green-bean casserole added sweet and salty flavors to the meal. Crisp and crunchy tossed salad sits along the side with dressings too numerous to list. Before dessert even arrived, everyone was already overfull. Still, they dined on sumptuous pumpkin pie. Its rich texture, with the tastes of cinnamon and pumpkin, was the perfect conclusion to the meal. Everyone had a great time at Grandma's house this Thanksgiving.

2. *Discuss your evaluation with your instructor.*

Day 3

A. **Formality Drill:**
Using the formality and grammar rules explained in Lesson 2, rewrite the sentence below in proper form:

Even though all the fans were on high, the family couldn't find a cool spot.

B. **Lesson Exercise:**
1. *Based on the guidelines given in this week's lesson, critique the following paragraph, marking scores, comments, and corrections on a grading form copied from Appendix E.*

   Assignment: define obedience
   Type of paragraph: definition paragraph
   Purpose: inform
   Audience: a peer, who needs to understand the term

   Obedience is very important. The dictionary says that obedience means doing what one is told (World Book). In almost every job, a level of obedience is required. In the home, children need to obey their parents. Many books tell of bad consequences for those who don't obey. For example, almost everyone has heard of the need to obey the Ten Commandments. These rules help us all to treat one another better. If we don't obey them, bad things can happen to us like: being grounded, being punished, other people being mad at us, being put in jail, and worse. Clearly, obedience is very important in order to avoid bad things.

2. Discuss your evaluation with your instructor.

Day 4

A. **Grammar Drill:**
Continue reviewing the prepositions.

B. **Style Drill:**
Identify the style point used in the following sentence.

Thirstily, the boy drank the entire bottle of water.

C. **Lesson Exercise:**
1. *Based on the guidelines given in this week's lesson, critique the following paragraph, marking scores, comments, and corrections on a grading form copied from Appendix E.*

Assignment: describe an event or setting
Type of paragraph: descriptive paragraph
Purpose: to persuade
Audience: someone who missed the event

Recently, I attended my parents' fiftieth wedding anniversary reception. As soon as I entered the building, I noticed the roses and candles which decorated the place. Some sort of netting was spread over cream tablecloths. On top of this sat the decorations. In the front of the room were three tables with beverages, cake, and fruit and vegetable trays. You should have heard the loud noise that reached my ears as people, who had not seen one another in a long time, greeted one another. Seventeen tables were spread all throughout the room, and next to them were white chairs for people to sit in. When visitors entered the room, they greeted my mom and dad before they got some snacks. Along the wall on the left side of the room were display boards which displayed family photos. Her wedding gown and his suit were hung on display boards. Although aged over the fifty years, the satin gown still shown with a warm hue, and the blue suit was of a vintage, nineteen-fifties style. Punch in the crystal punch bowl was a raspberry pink hue. Not too many people took coffee because the room was warm from outside heat and the large number of people filling the room. Three, lovely ladies worked hard to serve the cake, pour the punch, and refill trays. Everyone seemed to have a lovely time at this exciting event — mostly my parents.

2. *Discuss your evaluation with your instructor.*

Day 5

A. Formality Drill:

Using the formality and grammar rules explained in Lesson 2, rewrite the sentence below in proper form:

When George Washington was young, his dad died, so his mom and his brother, Lawrence, played the most influential roles in his life.

B. Lesson Exercise:

1. *Based on the guidelines given in this week's lesson, critique the following paragraph, marking scores, comments, and corrections on a grading form copied from Appendix E.*

   Assignment: describe a scene
   Type of paragraph: descriptive paragraph
   Purpose: to persuade
   Audience: someone who might have liked to see the scene

   The scenery snowboarding down Mount Hood is spectacular. On both sides of the downhill slope are lush, green, snow-covered, pine trees. When the wind blows, the trees sway back and forth, making a light swishing sound. The snow, which glistens in the sunlight like glitter, is soft, clean, and white. Because of the temperature and snow, the air is invigoratingly damp and chilly. When snowboarding down the mountain, the chilly wind beating against one's face gives a considerable chill. One also hears a slight, crackling noise from the snowboard gliding over the snow. The scenic, winter landscape on Mount Hood draws many to experience it.

2. *Discuss your evaluation with your instructor.*

WEEK 13
Descriptive Paragraphs, Definition Paragraphs, and Thinking Like a Teacher (continued)

Daily Assignments

Day 1

A. Lesson Exercise:
1. *Based on the guidelines given in Week 12 Lesson, critique the following paragraph, marking scores, comments, and corrections on a grading form copied from Appendix E.*

   Assignment: describe an event
   Type of paragraph: descriptive paragraph
   Purpose: to persuade
   Audience: someone who might have liked to see the event

      At the Children's Theatre, Charlotte saw the best play that she had ever seen. The atmosphere in the theater was charged with expectancy. Play goers shuffled quietly to their seats and settled down into the semi-darkened environment. The vintage, wooden seats squeaked as they were pushed into horizontal position. In front of creative backdrops, the March family's story began to unfold. The play revolved around Jo March, the central character, and her three sisters. Charlotte's affinity for the play started with an appreciation of the sisterly bond among the March girls since she had two delightful sisters of her own. This young play-goer saw how the March girls sacrificed their own wishes to be kind to their mother and father. Jo, Charlotte's favorite character, even cut her long hair and sold it in order to provide her mother with the train fare to go care for the family's ailing father. Jo's sacrifices extended to her sisters as well. For instance, when the young suitor in whom Jo is interested seems to have affection for her sister, Jo moves to New York to allow the relationship between the two to develop. Most significantly, Charlotte's favorite aspect of the play was Jo's aspirations to be a writer. As an aspiring writer herself, Charlotte enjoyed watching Jo progress from publishing her first work, to becoming a successful writer. Almost as a reward for Jo's selflessness, she met a professor in New York whom she ultimately marries. Therefore, Charlotte most loved this play because of the spunky, creative, selfless character of Jo.

2. *Discuss that evaluation with your instructor.*

Day 2

A. Writing Exercise:
Based on your instructor's feedback, you will begin an edit week, reworking the descriptive paragraph which you wrote in Week 9. (Instructor's option: Have student also edit the definition paragraph written in Week 11.) Today, edit all form, structure, and logic problems in the paragraph. This includes points off topic, unsupported contentions, and all other points in the top section of the grading form. If necessary, make a new planning outline and rewrite portions which are not correct. Additionally, do more research as needed in order to present your points more adequately.

Day 3

A. Writing Exercise:
Today, continue editing your descriptive (definition) paragraph by correcting stylistic and impression problems. This includes sentence variety, emphasis, transitions, and all other parts in "Impression" portion of grading form.

Day 4

A. Writing Exercise:
Today, correct any mechanical errors in your paragraph. This includes grammar, spelling, punctuation, and informalities. Also, prepare all items needed with your re-submission, including anything not submitted the first time.

Day 5

A. Writing Exercise:
1. *Again, read your work aloud and be certain that you have improved in every area which the instructor has deemed necessary. Rewrite a final draft of your paragraph.*
2. *Submit:*
    a. *Your rewritten paragraph.*
    b. *Any other rewritten items – ie. brainstorming, outline, etc.*
    c. *The evaluation form which your instructor completed.*
    d. *The paragraph on which your teacher wrote corrections.*
    e. *Any items which you did not submit with your first paragraph.*

B. Test:
Complete Week 13 Quiz over Week 9, Week 10, and Week 11 Lessons.

WEEK 14

Lesson: *Narrative Paragraphs*

14.1 Introduction

Narrative paragraphs simply tell a story or relay a sequence of events. Generally, these events are told in chronological order; that is, the order in which they happened. However, a narrative paragraph most often tells a story in order to illustrate or demonstrate a point. Because of this, developing a strong topic sentence is important. For instance, the following topic sentence would be considered weak for a narrative paragraph:

> *Jeff's family went on a fishing trip to Horning's Hideout.*

The above topic sentence lacks appeal and leaves the reader thinking, "So what!" because the sentence has not established any purpose for the paragraph.

14.2 Purpose and Appeal

Sometimes narrative writing can simply entertain the reader; however, in formal academic writing, the purpose of a narrative paragraph is to inform or persuade. To add purpose, the **topic sentence** should establish a contention which the author will set out to prove in the paragraph. In so doing, he adds appeal as well. The following topic sentence stands in contrast to the one above:

> *Fishing at Horning's Hideout proved to be an enjoyable outing for Jeff and his family.*

This sentence makes an assertion to be proven in the paragraph and is more appealing to the reader. Yes, the paragraph will tell the story of the family's fishing trip, but it will do so in a way which proves the trip to have been enjoyable. Furthermore, establishing a contention improves appeal by challenging the reader to respond to what is said. Finally, establishing this topic sentence limits the perspective or angle which will be taken on the subject. Now supporting information must be developed.

14.3 Developing a narrative paragraph

All the enjoyable parts of the family fishing trip have been established as the topic of this narrative paragraph. Hence, the writer can brainstorm supporting information with a clear goal in mind. An extensive list of enjoyable parts for everyone should be developed. Most likely, all of these will not be used, but any points which might serve to support the contention must be considered. Illustration 14A below is a list of as many pleasant aspects of the trip as the writer could recall.

Following the brainstorming of supporting information, the writer must develop a planning outline, such as in Illustration 14B, for using this material. The outline will help one stay logical and topical as points are organized into related

Narrative paragraphs tell a story or relay a sequence of events.

The topic sentence of a narrative paragraph does not start the narration. It establishes a purpose.

groupings. Naturally with a narrative paragraph, points are arranged in chronological order.

14A - Brainstorming Supporting Information

Contention:	*Trip was enjoyable*
All:	*Excited preparations for the trip* *- Food, games, books, toys, fishing equipment* *Great place to fish* *Fun being in the woods* *Great weather*
Jeff and brother:	*Purchased bait there* *Catching the fish was fun* *Caught seven fish* *Interesting to see white peacocks* *Time with Father*
Father:	*Family time, tasty dinner*
Mother:	*Did needlework, read book, had quiet time*

The student will notice that the ideas above are reorganized into chronological order in the planning outline.

Events in narrative paragraphs should be arranged chronologically.

14B - Planning Outline

Topic sentence - The family enjoyed the trip.
1. *Preparations*
   a. *Mother - food, books, needlework*
   b. *Father - car*
   c. *Boys - fishing poles, toys, books*
2. *Reach destination*
   a. *Purchase bait*
3. *Finding fishing spot*
   a. *Finding first place*
   b. *Moving to second place*
4. *Real fishing began*
   a. *Brother caught fish*
   b. *Jeff caught fish*
   c. *Father busy*
      (1) *Helping boys cast*
      (2) *Helping keep hooks baited*
      (3) *Helping reel in catch*
   d. *Mother read and did needlework*
   e. *Caught seven fish*
   f. *Cleaned fish before leaving*
5. *Jeff and brother were excited to catch fish*
6. *Father enjoyed time with sons*
7. *Mother enjoyed quiet time*

Concluding sentence - It was fun for all.

14C - Sample Paragraph

> *Fishing Fun*
>
> *Fishing at Horning's Hideout proved to be an enjoyable outing for Jeff and his family. All family members rose early in the morning excited to prepare for the trip. Mother packed food for the family as well as her books and needlework. Father checked the car to make certain it was ready for the drive. Then with Father's help, Jeff and his brother readied their fishing poles along with the books and toys which would entertain them on the hour's drive. When the family arrived at their destination, they stopped by the office to purchase some worms to use as bait. Cheerfully walking along the narrow path, the family transported their gear all the way around the small pond looking for just the right place to cast their lines. In hopes that fish would be lurking in the shadows, Jeff and his brother decided to fish from a shady area along one side of the pond. Though it seemed like the perfect fishing spot, overhead branches interfered with casting. Undaunted after snagging lines several times, the avid fishermen decided it would be best to move to the other side of the pond. Here, the fish began to bite. Before long, Jeff's older brother caught the first fish. Jeff caught one soon after. Suddenly, Father became very active, helping the two excited boys keep their hooks baited and reel in catch after catch. Just before noon, Jeff hooked what turned out to be the largest trout of the day, which he hung in the water near the shore with the other captured fish. While Father and the boys fished, Mother enjoyed sitting at the picnic table and reading quietly or doing her needlework. After several hours of fishing, and a total catch of seven fish, Father showed the boys how to clean the fish before packing up for the trip home. The outing was great fun for the whole family. Jeff and his brother found much excitement in catching the fish. Father enjoyed helping the boys and spending a day in the woods. Mother expressed her pleasure in being with her family and seeing everyone having an agreeable time. Most of all, everyone's taste buds were delighted with the dinner that evening. Because the day was such fun, the family is hoping for a return trip soon.*

14.4 Using dialogue in the narrative

Since students tend to include dialogue in a narrative paragraph, they should understand the two ways to present discourse. The first method is direct discourse or dialogue which is a quote of the exact words spoken by someone. These words, when written exactly as spoken, are to be presented in quotation marks and attributed to the speaker. The second method of presenting dialogue is indirect discourse by which the words are paraphrased and not written in quotation marks. This is the method students are to use in assignments for this course when recounting personal experience. This limitation, however, does not apply when presenting research material.

Below are samples of direct and indirect discourse which the student should study to learn how to change from one form to the other.

Direct Discourse (Dialogue)	Indirect Discourse
"I had a delightful time with my family and so appreciated everyone getting along with one another," said Mother on the way home.	Mother expressed her pleasure in being with her family and seeing everyone having an agreeable time.
Jason suggested, "Let's move to the other side of the pond."	Jason calmly suggested that the family move to another side of the pond.

Literary Device

Figurative language, as mentioned in Lesson 8, explains one concept or item with another in order to clarify the first. The **metaphor** is one such literary device practiced in this lesson. Like a simile, a metaphor compares two items; but instead of saying one thing is "like" another, it treats the one as if it _is_ the other. For example:

> Flowing water <u>sliced</u> through the dike.
> The farmer touched the <u>hot</u> fence to see if the <u>juice</u> was flowing.

A metaphor compares two items without the use of "like" or "as."

The student should note that metaphorical wording does not include "like" or "as." The writer of the above sentences does not spell out that water is acting like a knife, or that an electrified fence feels like it is hot, or that voltage is as juice. Instead, he leaves it up to the reader's mind to connect each pair of concepts.

Metaphors occur frequently and can be found in a variety of parts of speech. The student should study the following chart to become familiar with some of the many uses of metaphors.

verbs:	The game <u>heated up</u> as the quarterback <u>rifled</u> the pass to the receiver who <u>knifed</u> between two defenders and "<u>tightroped</u>" down the sideline. After much negotiation, the salesman <u>shaved</u> ten percent off the price of the car.
adjectives and adverbs:	Life is a <u>carnival</u> ride. The <u>ferocious</u> housecat attacked its prey. The quarterback threw the football to the <u>flying</u> receiver.
prepositional phrases:	He had muscles (of <u>steel</u>.) She was saddened (by her <u>ash heap</u>) of dreams.
nouns:	The <u>army</u> of seals swam in <u>ranks</u>. Her decorative <u>touch</u> was evident in the home.
appositives:	On the bed sat the dog, a <u>whining baby</u>.

WEEK 14
Narrative Paragraphs

Daily Assignments

——— Day 1 ———

A. Reading Assignment:
Study the Week 14 Lesson on narrative paragraphs thoroughly.

B. Lesson Exercise:
Answer the following questions in complete sentences:

1. What must be established in order to make a narrative paragraph interesting?
2. What are the two methods for presenting dialogue?
3. What is a metaphor?

C. Writing Exercise:
1. *Brainstorm a narrative paragraph on a topic approved by your instructor. Write your brainstorming list neatly, in a manner that is suitable for submission with your final draft.*
    Purpose: inform
    Audience: peers
    Topic suggestions: a family outing, a family crisis

2. *Do research, if required, for supporting information. Gather bibliographic information, general notes on the topic, and prepare quotations, summaries, or paraphrases to offer in support of your position as described in the Week 10 Lesson.*

3. *Write a topic sentence and create a planning outline for this narrative paragraph. The planning outline will also be submitted to your instructor with your final draft.*

——— Day 2 ———

A. Grammar Drill:
Review the prepositions.

B. Style Drill:
Identify the style point used in the following sentence.

   While Thomas Jefferson and Patrick Henry both participated in Virginia colonial politics, the men differed greatly.

C. Writing Exercise:
Draft the entire narrative paragraph which you planned on Day 1. Insert proper citations for any research evidence included. This week's literary device, a metaphor, is to be

included in the paragraph and may be added any time between now and Day 4. If you find, at this point, that your planning outline must be changed, revise it and create a new copy for submission.

Complete a copy of your paragraph draft today so that you can mark corrections on it tomorrow. This draft, with corrections, will be submitted to your instructor with your final draft on Day 5.

Day 3

A. Grammar Drill:
Drill the prepositions again.

B. Formality Drill:
Using the formality and grammar rules explained in Lesson 2, rewrite the sentence below in proper form:

Jefferson didn't like making speeches or participating in oral dispute.

C. Writing Exercise:
1. *Now begin to edit your paragraph draft from yesterday, marking corrections and changes on your rough draft. Consult the paragraph checklist to insure that you are following set guidelines.*
2. *Add three different style points on this day.*
3. *Create another copy of this revision for submission on Day 5.*

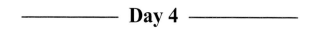

Day 4

A. Grammar Drill:
Drill the prepositions. Now write the list in order from memory and submit it to your instructor for correction.

B. Style Drill:
Identify the style point used in the following sentence.

In contrast, Patrick Henry's reputation as an outstanding orator still stands today.

C. Writing Exercise:
1. *Go over your paragraph and correct all spelling, punctuation, and grammatical errors.*
2. *This week's literary device must be added to the paragraph by this day. If you cannot fit the device into the assignment, write two sample sentences, each including this week's literary device, and submit them with your paragraph.*
3. *Make other improvements in words and phrases that may come to mind.*
4. *Prepare a revised draft of your paragraph.*

Day 5

A. Grammar Drill:
Drill prepositions again today.

B. Formality Drill:
Using the formality and grammar rules explained in Lesson 2, rewrite the sentence below in proper form:

Since both Jefferson and Henry opposed George III and the British Parliament.

C. Writing Exercise:
1. *The final day to polish your paragraph has come. Read the paragraph aloud slowly and listen for problem areas. Now, have someone else read it to you so that you can listen and be certain that the product is well-written.*

2. *Using the Paragraph Checklist, review your paragraph. Check off each guideline in the upper section when you have verified that you have followed it. In the lower section, mark the style points you have used. On your final draft, identify these style points by writing the corresponding number from the checklist directly above each one, and label the literary device.*

3. *Make certain that the text includes appropriate parenthetical citations in-text, and that the "Works Cited" page is complete.*

4. *Make certain that the assignment is formatted properly, including heading.*

5. *Submit your work to the instructor:*
    a. *Final draft paragraph*
    b. *"Works Cited" page, if applicable*
    c. *Literary device, if created separately*
    d. *Paragraph checklist*
    e. *All drafts*
    f. *Topic sentence & planning outline*
    g. *Brainstorming*

WEEK 15
Narrative Paragraphs (continued)

Daily Assignments

────────── **Day 1** ──────────

A. Grammar Drill:
Drill the prepositions.

B. Formality Drill:
Using the formality and grammar rules explained in Lesson 2, rewrite the sentence below in proper form:

> Benjamin Franklin and John Adams, who were also appointed to draft the Declaration of Independence, suggested ideas but didn't write the final draft.

C. Writing Exercise:
This week you will prepare for a timed writing of a narrative paragraph on Day 5. To prepare for the paragraph, you will do research, gather bibliographic information, prepare general notes on the topic, and prepare quotations, summaries, or paraphrases to offer in support of your position as described in Week 10. Today, brainstorm possible contentions for your topic sentence. Next, gather the sources needed for your research. Citings from at least two sources will be required.

> *Purpose: to inform in an entertaining manner*
> *Type of paragraph: narrative*
> *Audience: peers who might not know about this event*
> *Suggested topic: a historical event (NO FICTION)*

────────── **Day 2** ──────────

A. Grammar Drill:
Drill the prepositions.

B. Style Drill:
Identify the style point used in the following sentence.

> Knowing Jefferson to be the better writer, Franklin and Adams deferred to him.

C. Writing Exercise:
1. *From a minimum of two sources, take general notes as needed on the topic and obtain at least six quotes, summaries, or paraphrases.*
2. *Develop a list of the bibliographic information which corresponds to your notes. On the*

day you write your paragraph, you will draw from this list for your "Works Cited" page. Naturally, only the sources you cite in your paragraph will be cited on the "Works Cited" page. General or common knowledge gleaned from your sources need not be specifically cited.

Day 3

A. Grammar Drill:
Drill the prepositions.

B. Formality Drill:
Using the formality and grammar rules explained in Lesson 2, rewrite the sentence below in proper form:

When Tom was asked to write the Declaration of Independence, he took up the challenge willingly.

C. Writing Exercise:
1. *Complete your research.*
2. *Brainstorm supporting points from your research and your own knowledge about the topic.*
3. *Formulate a final topic sentence and complete a planning outline for your paragraph.*

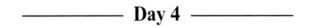
Day 4

A. Grammar Drill:
Drill the prepositions.

B. Style Drill:
Identify the style point used in the following sentence.

Clearly, both Jefferson and Henry possessed their own special talents.

C. Writing Exercise:
1. *Of the quotes you have compiled, <u>you may use only two</u> in this paragraph. The remainder of the paragraph must be your own writing. Today, determine which quotes you will use and where they will fit into the planning outline. <u>You may not pre-write your paragraph.</u>*
2. *Create a Working Bibliography for all the sources you studied. <u>Do not create the "Works Cited" page</u>. It will be written during the timed write on Day 5.*

3. *Gather all materials which you will need for tomorrow's timed write:*
    a. *Note cards*
    b. *Topic sentence and planning outline*
    c. *Working Bibliography page*
    d. *Brainstorming*

―――――― **Day 5** ――――――

A. Grammar Drill:
Drill prepositions again today.

B. Formality Drill:
Using the formality and grammar rules explained in Lesson 2, rewrite the sentence below in proper form:

> Jefferson wasn't home from France very long before Washington asked him to serve as Secretary of State.

C. Writing Exercise:
Today's exercise will be a 30-minute timed write.

1. *Using your notes and planning outline, write a narrative paragraph on your chosen topic. Strive for ten to twelve sentences, but the paragraph may be longer if desired. Be certain to include two parenthetical references in the paragraph.*

    Audience: peers who might not know about this event
    Purpose: to inform in an entertaining manner

2. *Develop a "Works Cited" page for your sources. It should be organized according to MLA guidelines. You may refer back to the Week 10 Lesson and to the documentation formats in Appendix D on page 202.*

3. *When the time is up, submit the following to your instructor:*
    a. *Written paragraph*
    b. *"Works Cited" page*
    c. *Working Bibliography page*
    d. *Planning outline*
    e. *Brainstorming*
    f. *Note cards*

WEEK 16
Narrative Paragraphs (continued)

Daily Assignments

Day 1

A. Reading Assignment:
Re-read *the Week 14 Lesson on narrative paragraphs.*

B. Formality Drill:
Using the formality and grammar rules explained in Lesson 2, rewrite the sentence below in proper form:

Jefferson penned the Declaration of Independence and leaves his own legacy.

C. Writing Exercise:
1. *Based on the guidelines given in Week 12 Lesson, critique the following paragraph, marking scores, comments, and corrections on a grading form copied from Appendix E.*

   Assignment: tell of an event
   Type of paragraph: narrative paragraph
   Purpose: to persuade
   Audience: instructor

   The Fourth of July fireworks show at Fort Stevens proved to be a delightful outing with special friends. The Barrett's first preparation for the outing was to invite their special friends, the Millers, to enjoy the fireworks with them. After the families agreed to meet at the fort, each Barrett family member began his own preparations for the outing. One day before the outing, Mom started first with food preparations as she cooked potatoes for salad and prepared finger foods which insured light and healthy eating. Finally, the day of the event, she cut up bite-sized chunks of delicious summer fruits. The boys gathered frisbees, balls, hacky sacks, and other playthings. Next, Dad pulled the cooler, lawn chairs, and blankets out of storage. Preparations were also underway in the Miller home as the mother fried tasty chicken, baked crusty French bread, and whipped up a delectable berry dessert. Both families loaded their cars with goodies expecting a great time of food and fellowship. When they reached the fort, the families walked close to a mile to reach their destination. Then they spread their blankets on the ground and set up lawn chairs around the perimeter. Then all around them, other families "staked claim to their territories" in order to secure a great view of the fireworks show. Next came the waiting for darkness to fall. Food and frolic filled these moments of fleeting daylight. The boys played hacky sack and catch until they lost a favorite ball in a nearby tree. Then, at long last, daylight waned and the fireworks show began. Background music being broadcast from a local radio station blared over hundreds of radios which had been brought by spectators. Then, choreographed to this background accompaniment, a spectacular display began. Sparkling, dazzling, creative combinations of explosions filled the night sky. So powerful were the fireworks, that the spectators felt the concussion of their explosions. Patriotic music rose above the explosive din. Then, with a stellar finale of a multitude of fireworks, the grand presentation ended. Rapidly, all began to gather belongings in order to embark on the trek back to their vehicles. The evening spent with fellowship, food, and fireworks proved to be a memory which both families will treasure.

2. Discuss your evaluation with your instructor.

Day 2

A. Style Drill:
Identify the style point used in the following sentence.

The Second Continental Congress appointed Jefferson, who represented Virginia, to draft a formal statement regarding the colonies' break with Great Britain.

B. Writing Exercise:
Based on your instructor's feedback, you will begin an edit week, reworking the narrative paragraph which you wrote in Week 14. Today, edit all form, structure, and logic problems in the paragraph. This includes points off topic, unsupported contentions, and all other points in the top section of grading form. If necessary, make a new planning outline and rewrite portions which are not correct. Additionally, do more research as needed in order to present your points more adequately.

Day 3

A. Formality Drill:
Using the formality and grammar rules explained in Lesson 2, rewrite the sentence below in proper form:

Jefferson was chosen to be president in a tie-breaking vote by the House of Representatives.

B. Writing Exercise:
Today, continue editing your narrative paragraph by correcting stylistic and impression problems. This includes sentence variety, emphasis, transitions, and all other parts in the "Impression" portion of grading form.

Day 4

A. Style Drill:
Identify the style point used in the following sentence.

In favor of the Louisiana Purchase was Thomas Jefferson.

B. Writing Exercise:
Today, correct any mechanical errors in your paragraph. This includes grammar, spelling, punctuation, and informalities. Also, prepare all items needed with your re-submission, including anything not submitted the first time.

Day 5

A. Grammar Drill:
Again, rehearse the prepositions.

B. Formality Drill:
Using the formality and grammar rules explained in Lesson 2, rewrite the sentence below in proper form:

   Jefferson served as governor of Virginia. Prior to his becoming president.

C. Writing Exercise:
1. *Again, read your work aloud and be certain that you have improved in every area which the instructor has deemed necessary. Rewrite a final draft of your paragraph.*
2. *Submit:*
    a. *Your rewritten paragraph.*
    b. *Any other rewritten items – ie. brainstorming, outline, etc.*
    c. *The evaluation form filled out by your instructor.*
    d. *The paragraph on which your teacher wrote corrections.*
    e. *Any items which you did not submit with your first paragraph.*

WEEK 17

Lesson: *Process Paragraphs*

17.1 Introduction

The paragraph that explains sequential steps is called a **process paragraph**. A well-written paragraph of this type should describe the steps so clearly that the reader can *exactly* copy them if he desires. Great attention to detail, precise use of words, and logical order are required.

17.2 Development

Once again, the topic sentence should identify the process to be explained and include a contention in order to set the tone for the paragraph:

Using a telephone calling card is a simple process.

Besides stating the process, the above sentence sets an objective of convincing the reader of its simplicity. Establishing this objective is important. To make this type of paragraph creative and interesting, the contention must state more than an obvious fact about the process itself. An opinion or perspective on the process should be offered.

After the objective is set, the writer must assume that the reader is not familiar with the process and describe precisely what happens and when. Therefore, the planning outline and paragraph should follow chronological order. In nearly every process, the three phases of preparation, action, and completion should be addressed. For example, if the reader needs to prepare for the project by gathering materials or ingredients, that should be explained prior to describing the action steps involved. Next, each step in the action phase should be first introduced, then accurately described and explained. The writer must not assume any details to be understood without full explanation. In some instances, it may even be necessary to explain what to do if circumstances do not go as planned. The completion phase discusses the finalization of the process. Lastly, the concluding sentence reiterates the original contention and may include an interesting comment or observation. With a thoroughly developed outline, explaining a process should come readily.

A process paragraph explains a sequence of steps.

17A - Sample Process Outline

> *Contention: Simple process*
> 1. *Begin call*
>   a. *Dial 800 number found on back of card*
> 2. *Follow recorded instructions*
>   a. *Choose language*
>   b. *Enter identification number from card*
>   c. *Select national or international type call*
>   d. *Dial the intended phone number*
>
> *Conclusion - Connection, conversation begins*

17B - Sample Process Paragraph

> *Using a telephone calling card only requires a few simple steps. Once the calling card is procured, it is time to begin the call. Printed on the back of the card will be an 800 number which the caller must first dial. When the automated service answers, simple step-by-step instructions begin to play. The caller is asked to choose instructions in a desired language. If one wants to receive directions in English or Spanish, a specified key on the phone must be pressed. Step three involves entering an identification number. The caller locates it on the back of the calling card. Fourth, the dialer must indicate whether the call will be national or international. Again, pressing the number option listed in the recorded commands establishes the proper link. Lastly, the caller dials the phone number of the party he intends to contact. By following these simple directions, the connection is made and conversation begins.*

17.3 Avoid mixing persons

One of students' most common errors with a process paragraph is the mixing of persons in the subject of the sentences. Many students combine imperative sentences, in which the subject is an understood or implied "you," with sentences which say "one should..." or "he should..." To do this creates a shift in person and is, therefore, grammatically incorrect because the person must remain the same through the entire paragraph or essay.

First person:
I, me, we, us

Second person:
you, your

Third person:
he, she, they, one

17C - Examples of Shifts in Person

Incorrect:	*Next, the <u>chef</u> combines the eggs with all liquid ingredients in the blender. <u>One</u> should blend them on high for two minutes. Then (<u>you</u>) pour the mixture over the dry ingredients.*
Correction 1: (Not appropriate if formality is required.)	*Next, fill the blender with the eggs and all liquid ingredients. Blend them on high for two minutes, then pour the mixture over the dry ingredients.* (These are imperative sentences with an understood "you" as the subject.)
Correction 2:	*Next, the chef fills the blender with all liquid ingredients. She should blend them on high for two minutes. When fully blended, she pours the mixture over the dry ingredients.*

A simple way to solve this common grammatical error is to write as if a fictional character is performing the task. If this is not proper for the assignment given, make certain that all of the subjects remain consistent. The following well written process paragraph uses a fictional character in Illustration 17D.

17D - Process Paragraph with Fictional Character

> *With careful planning, John Morris writes a concise paragraph. First, he brainstorms the direction and the supporting details of the paragraph. When brainstorming the direction, John writes down specific topic ideas. After choosing a subject, he lists the supporting details he will use in the paragraph. Next, John outlines his paragraph. He wisely places each idea correctly, showing subordinating and coordinating thoughts. The next step is writing the rough draft. John strives to use strong verbs. He endeavors to write a concise topic and concluding sentence. Following the rough draft stage, John revises his composition. He carefully checks for unclear words, phrases, and sentences. In addition, John searches for grammatical errors. Finally, John Morris proofreads his paragraph, making sure he has the proper form. From writing a good topic sentence to eliminating contractions, John scrutinizes every question on his checklist. After printing the final copy, John Morris presents his paragraph to his mother.*
>
> Written by Patrick Gay, age 11, Tigard, Oregon
> Copyright 2001 Patrick Gay, All Rights Reserved - Used by permission

17.4 Literary Device

Employment of figurative language will again be used in this lesson. Two techniques, which are the opposite of one another, will be practiced. The first is **understatement**. The understatement presents material with deliberate control or constraint for emphasis. In contrast, the opposite of this is **hyperbole (overstatement)** which is an exaggeration for deliberate effect. Consider the following examples:

An understatement presents material with deliberate restraint for emphasis.

Understatement: Honey, the fender of the car just has a tiny dent.

Justin "hardly broke a sweat" when he ran the marathon.

Hyperbole: This is the worst hyperbole ever written.

He was told "a million times" not to exaggerate.

A hyperbole is an exaggeration for deliberate effect.

These devices must be used with care. Both understatement and hyperbole make inaccurate statements of fact. Therefore, these techniques may not be used in a topic or concluding sentence because the contention would not be provable.

WEEK 17
Process Paragraphs

Daily Assignments

──────── Day 1 ────────

A. Reading Assignment:
Study the Week 17 Lesson on process paragraphs thoroughly.

B. Lesson Exercise:
Answer the following questions in complete sentences:
1. How clearly should a process paragraph explain the steps in a procedure?
2. What is a common error for writers of process paragraphs?
3. What is a hyperbole? What is an understatement?

C. Writing Exercise:
1. Brainstorm a process paragraph on a topic approved by your instructor. Prepare your brainstorming list neatly, in a manner that is suitable for submission with your final draft.

   Purpose: inform
   Audience: instructor choice
   Topic suggestions: a scientific process, steps for preparing a food or craft, steps in a mechanical process.

2. Do research as needed for supporting information. Gather bibliographic information, general notes on the topic, and prepare quotations, summaries, or paraphrases to offer in support of your position as described in the Week 10 Lesson.

3. Write a topic sentence and create a planning outline for this process paragraph. The planning outline will also be submitted to your instructor with your final draft.

──────── Day 2 ────────

A. Style Drill:
Identify the style point used in the following sentence.

John Adams, who was George Washington's vice-president, became the second president.

B. Writing Exercise:
Draft the entire process paragraph which you planned on Day 1. Insert proper citations for any research evidence included. This week's literary device, an understatement or a

hyperbole, is to be included in the paragraph and may be added any time between now and Day 4. If you find, at this point, that your planning outline must be changed, revise it and write a new copy for submission.

Create a copy of your paragraph so that you can mark corrections on it tomorrow. This draft, with corrections, will be submitted to your instructor with your final draft on Day 5.

Day 3

A. Formality Drill:
Using the formality and grammar rules explained in Lesson 2, rewrite the sentence below in proper form:

A lot of people favored George Washington for president.

B. Writing Exercise:
1. *Now begin to edit your paragraph draft from yesterday, marking corrections and changes on your rough draft. Consult the paragraph checklist to ensure that you are following set guidelines.*

2. *Add three different style points on this day.*

3. *If you are working on the computer, create another copy of this revision for submission on Day 5.*

Day 4

A. Style Drill:
Identify the style point used in the following sentence.

Believing that the Supreme Court did not have ultimate right of judicial review, Jefferson opposed Chief Justice John Marshall.

B. Writing Exercise:
1. *Go over your paragraph and correct all spelling, punctuation, and grammatical errors.*

2. *This week's literary device, <u>either</u> an understatement or a hyperbole, must be added to the paragraph by this day. Again, if you cannot fit the device into the assignment, write two sample sentences, each including this week's literary device and submit them with your paragraph.*

3. *Make other improvements in words and phrases that may come to mind.*

4. *Prepare a revised draft of your paragraph.*

Day 5

A. Grammar Drill:
Rehearse the prepositions again today so that you continue to remember them.

B. Formality Drill:
Using the formality and grammar rules explained in Lesson 2, rewrite the sentence below in proper form:

When Jefferson was in office, he disagree with Alexander Hamilton.

C. Writing Exercise:

1. *The final day to polish your paragraph has come. Read the paragraph aloud slowly and listen for problem areas. Now, have someone else read it to you so that you can listen and be certain that the product is well-written.*

2. *Using the Paragraph Checklist, review your paragraph. Check off each guideline in the upper section when you have verified that you have followed it. In the lower section, mark the style points you have used. On your final draft, identify these style points by writing the corresponding number from the checklist directly above each one and label the literary device.*

3. *Make certain that the text includes appropriate parenthetical references in-text and that the "Works Cited" page is complete.*

4. *Make certain that the assignment is properly formatted.*

5. *Submit your work to the instructor:*

    a. *Final draft paragraph*
    b. *"Works Cited" page, as applicable*
    c. *Literary device, if not included in paragraph*
    d. *Paragraph checklist*
    e. *All drafts*
    f. *Topic sentence & planning outline*
    g. *Brainstorming*

WEEK 18
Process Paragraphs (continued)

Daily Assignments

──────── **Day 1** ────────

A. Formality Drill:
Using the formality and grammar rules explained in Lesson 2, rewrite the sentence below in proper form: (2 errors)

Jim Madison also served as Secretary of State under President Tom Jefferson.

B. Writing Exercise:
This week you will prepare for a timed writing of a process paragraph on Day 5. To prepare for the paragraph, you will do research, gather bibliographic information, prepare general notes on the topic, and prepare quotations, summaries, or paraphrases to offer in support of your position as described in Week 10. Today, brainstorm possible contentions for your topic sentence. Next, gather the sources needed for your research. Citings from at least two sources will be required.

Topic: student choice
Purpose: inform
Audience: a younger student
Suggested ideas: photosynthesis, another scientific process, a craft project, a cooking project

──────── **Day 2** ────────

A. Style Drill:
Identify the style point used in the following sentence.

During Madison's presidency, America fought the War of 1812.

B. Writing Exercise:
1. From a minimum of two different sources, take general notes as needed on the topic and obtain at least six quotes, summaries, or paraphrases. The sources must be standard sources and not package labels, television commercials, newspaper advertisements, and the like.

2. Develop a list of the bibliographic information which corresponds to your notes. On the day you write your paragraph, you will draw from this list for your "Works Cited" page. Naturally, only the sources you use in your paragraph will be cited on the "Works Cited" page. General or common knowledge gleaned from your sources need not be specifically cited.

Day 3

A. Formality Drill:
Using the formality and grammar rules explained in Lesson 2, rewrite the sentence below in proper form:

Thomas Jefferson and John Adams both kicked the bucket on the fiftieth anniversary of the proclamation of the Declaration of Independence, the Fourth of July.

B. Writing Exercise:
1. *Complete your research.*
2. *Brainstorm supporting points from your research and your own knowledge about the topic.*
3. *Formulate a final topic sentence and develop a planning outline for your paragraph.*

Day 4

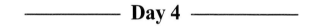

A. Style Drill:
Identify the style point used in the following sentence.

While Jefferson served as a diplomat in France, the Constitution was drafted and ratified.

B. Writing Exercise:
1. *Of the quotes you compiled, you may use only two in this paragraph. Today, determine which quotes you will use and where they will fit into the planning outline.* <u>You may not pre-write your paragraph.</u>
2. *Create a Working Bibliography for all the sources you studied.* <u>Do not create the "Works Cited" page.</u>
3. *Gather all materials which you will need for tomorrow's timed write:*
   a. *Note cards*
   b. *Topic sentence and planning outline*
   c. *Working Bibliography page*
   d. *Brainstorming*

Day 5

A. Grammar Drill:
Again, drill the prepositions.

B. Formality Drill:
Using the formality and grammar rules explained in Lesson 2, rewrite the sentence below in proper form:

You will find it hard to believe that both Jefferson and Adams died on such a significant day.

C. Writing Exercise:
Today's exercise will be a 30-minute timed write.

1. *Using your notes and planning outline, write a process paragraph on your chosen topic. Be certain to include two parenthetical references in the paragraph.*

    Audience: a younger student
    Purpose: inform

2. *Develop a "Works Cited" page for your sources. It should be organized according to MLA guidelines. You may refer back to the Week 10 Lesson and to the documentation formats in Appendix D on page 202.*

3. *When the time is up, submit the following to your instructor:*

    a. *Written paragraph*
    b. *"Works Cited" page*
    c. *Working Bibliography page*
    d. *Planning outline*
    e. *Notes, quotations, and other source material*

WEEK 19
Process Paragraphs (continued)

Daily Assignments

─────── **Day 1** ───────

A. Formality Drill:
Using the formality and grammar rules explained in Lesson 2, rewrite the sentence below in proper form:

Amazingly, the neighbor didn't recognize them.

B. Writing Exercise:
1. *Based on the guidelines given in Week 12 Lesson, critique the following paragraph, marking scores, comments, and corrections on a grading form copied from Appendix E.*

   Assignment: detail the making of gooey putty
   Type of paragraph: process
   Purpose: inform
   Audience: peers

   For Ashley and Olivia, creating gooey putty, for play, is an easy process. First, Ashley gathers the needed ingredients: 1 cup of white glue and 1 cup of liquid starch. She also retrieves a two-quart bowl in which to mix the putty. Olivia finds two aprons to protect their clothing and a spatula for mixing. Into the bowl, Olivia pours the white glue. Ashley begins to slowly add the liquid starch while Olivia stirs the mixture. Ashley stops pouring when the concoction becomes the consistency of putty. The girls soon begin to knead the putty with their hands to ensure a complete mixture. If the putty becomes too sticky, they add a little liquid starch. If is is not elastic enough, they add more glue. With the putty done, it is time for the play to begin. The girls spend the next half-hour squeezing the putty through their fingers and playing with the gooey mixture. Being such a simple process, they often create great enjoyment for themselves.

2. *Discuss your evaluation with your instructor.*

─────── **Day 2** ───────

A. Style Drill:
Identify the style point used in the following sentence.

To understand the works of Shakespeare, one needs to study their historical context.

B. Writing Exercise:
Based on your instructor's feedback, you will begin an edit week, reworking the process paragraph which you wrote in Week 17. Today, edit all form, structure, and logic problems

in the paragraph. This includes points off topic, unsupported contentions, and all other points in the top section of grading form. If necessary, make a new planning outline and rewrite portions which are not correct. Additionally, do more research as needed in order to present your points more adequately.

Day 3

A. Formality Drill:
Using the formality and grammar rules explained in Lesson 2, rewrite the sentence below in proper form:

Jacob went to the mall, and at the first store, they found the best birthday gift.

B. Writing Exercise:
Today, continue editing your process paragraph by correcting stylistic and impression problems. This includes sentence variety, emphasis, transitions, and all other parts in the "Impression" portion of grading form.

Day 4

A. Style Drill:
Identify the style point used in the following sentence.

Since he found the gift so rapidly, he stopped for a frozen yogurt treat.

B. Writing Exercise:
Today, correct any mechanical errors in your paragraph. This includes grammar, spelling, punctuation, and informalities. Also, prepare all items needed with your re-submission, including anything not submitted the first time.

Day 5

A. Grammar Drill:
Review the prepositions again.

B. Formality Drill:
Using the formality and grammar rules explained in Lesson 2, rewrite the sentence below in proper form:

The student was impressed by the study of the process of photosynthesis.

C. Writing Exercise:
  1. *Again, read your work aloud and be certain that you have improved in every area which the instructor has deemed necessary. Rewrite a final draft of your paragraph.*

2. *Submit:*
    a. *Your rewritten paragraph.*
    b. *Any other rewritten items – ie. brainstorming, outline, etc.*
    c. *The evaluation form filled out by your instructor.*
    d. *The paragraph on which your teacher wrote corrections.*
    e. *Any items which you did not submit with your first paragraph.*

D. Test:
Complete Week 19 Quiz over Week 14 and Week 17 Lessons.

WEEK 20

Lesson: *Comparison Paragraphs*

20.1 Introduction

A **comparison paragraph** discusses similarities or differences between items, concepts, or beliefs. Numerous items can be discussed; however, for a single paragraph it is best to compare only two items, or three at the most. The paragraph may be written either to inform or persuade and is developed in the following sequence.

A comparison paragraph evaluates similarities or differences.

20.2 Preliminary Considerations

A. *Topic*

For the comparison paragraph, the writer must make two preliminary decisions about the topic:

(1) Decide what to compare

(2) Determine the criteria for comparison

B. *Audience*

Identifying the audience must be the next critical step in writing this type of paragraph since the criteria for comparison and the conclusion will often differ depending on the needs of the readers. For example, if the assignment is to compare compact disc (CD) boom boxes, the writer must make certain assumptions about the desires of the potential audience. An older person may prefer the ability to play cassette tapes as well as CDs and have little need to use the boom box outside the home. On the other hand, today's teenager might have less interest in playing cassette tapes, preferring a unit which can be transported easily and with a bass boost. Hence, the criteria and conclusions in this instance will depend on whether the target audience will be older adults or teenagers.

C. *Purpose*

In comparison paragraphs, conclusions are generally given by the writer. However, the degree to which the writer tries to persuade his audience will vary from composition to composition. The author may simply be informing and reporting observations which lead to a conclusion. Other times, the paragraph writer may build a case for the conclusion and challenge the reader to accept the position or take action. Specific levels of persuasion for this assignment will be given by the instructor.

20.3 Planning

Illustration 20A shows how a simple comparison chart can be a helpful tool for planning a comparison paragraph.

20A - Comparison Chart

Target audience:	Teen who wants a portable "boom box"		
Criterion	**"Boom Box" A**	**"Boom Box" B**	**Conclusion**
Portability:	large size	compact size transportable	B is more portable
Sound:	fine sound	super sound base boost	Sound better from boom box B
Other features:	CD - 60 second anti-skip feature programmable AM/FM radio cassette tape player	CD - 30 second anti-skip feature programmable AM/FM radio	Other features better for boom box A
Cost:	$75.00	$60.00	Boom box B less expensive
Overall conclusion:	"Boom box" B is better - costs less, appealing sound for teen, transportable.		

20.4 Topic Sentence

An overall conclusion will form the basis for the topic sentence. This topic sentence may simply establish that two things are to be compared, or it may take a position that one is better than the other.

Comparison established:
- *When choosing between boom box A and boom box B, a number of features should be considered.*
- *Both boom box A and boom box B seem to be strong products worth considering.*

Position established:
- *Boom box B prevails over boom box A when evaluated on a number of features.*

20.5 Supporting Information and Concluding Sentence

The concluding sentence should summarize the author's reasons for preferring one option over the others.

For this type of paragraph, the writer must choose between two development options. In the first option, the writer may discuss, in turn, each comparison criterion as it pertains to the items. Conversely, each item may be discussed, covering all criteria about the first item before moving to the next. Regardless of the option selected, the writer should always present the supporting details in the same order and discuss the overall preferred item last. Finally, the concluding sentence should summarize the basis for the final selection. Based on the 20A Comparison Chart, the following two outlines detail both development options.

20B - Sample "Boom Box" Planning Outlines

Criterion Comparison Outline

Topic Sentence: When evaluated on a number of features, Boom Box B prevails over Boom Box A.
1. Portability
   a. Box A: large, heavy
   b. Box B: compact, transportable
2. Sound
   a. Box A: clear, strong
   b. Box B: superb, bass boost
3. Other features
   a. Box A: programmable, 60-second anti-skip, radio, cassette
   b. Box B: programmable, 30-second anti-skip, radio
4. Cost
   a. Box A: $75.00
   b. Box B: $60.00

Concluding Sentence

Item Comparison Outline

Topic Sentence: When evaluated on a number of features, Boom Box B prevails over Boom Box A.
1. Boom box A
   a. Portability: large, heavy
   b. Sound: clear, strong
   c. Other features: programmable, 60-second anti-skip, radio, cassette
   d. Cost: $75.00
2. Boom box B
   a. Portability: compact, transportable
   b. Sound: superb, bass boost
   c. Other features: programmable, 30-second anti-skip, radio
   d. Cost: $60.00

Concluding sentence

Comparison Development Options:
- **By item**
- **By criterion**

Presentation:
- **Organize supporting details in the same order.**
- **Discuss the overall preferred item last**

20C - Sample Comparison Paragraph by Criteria

After evaluating a number of features, Jeff selected the Blaring Barrett Boom Box over the Supersonic Square Sound System. Portability, Jeff's first requirement, seemed critical since he planned to take his boom box with him to the basketball courts. He studied the Barrett model, finding it to be smaller and lighter than the Supersonic. Naturally, sound became another consideration for Jeff. The sound from the Supersonic proved to be strong and clear, but when he noticed that the Barrett model came with a bass boost, that factor piqued his interest. Next, Jeff carefully examined other features. The Supersonic Square offered programmability, sixty-second anti-skip, AM/FM radio, and cassette tape player. In contrast, the Blaring Barrett came equipped with programmability, thirty-second anti-skip, and AM/FM radio. Analyzing the differences, Jeff realized that he rarely listened to cassette tapes, and the difference in the anti-skip feature was not significant to him. Jeff contemplated his final criterion: cost. With the two competitively priced, he saw that the Supersonic cost seventy-five dollars and the Barrett sold for sixty dollars. In this category, the Barrett model won again. At the end of the day, Blaring Barrett surpassed Supersonic Square based on portability, sound, and cost, so this astute young man chose that player.

20D - Sample Comparison Paragraph by Item

> *After evaluating a number of features, Jeff selected the Blaring Barrett Boom Box over the Supersonic Square Sound System. Sizing up the features of each model, Jeff noted aspects of the Supersonic. First, portability seemed problematic since it was large, sturdy, and had detachable speakers. Sound proved to be a second consideration. The Supersonic emitted balanced musical fidelity. Additional features, which this model offered, included programmability, sixty-second anti-skip, AM/FM radio, and cassette tape player. Finally, the Supersonic cost seventy-five dollars. Next, he weighed his options with the Blaring Barrett. Much more compact in size, and all in one unit, this seemed the better choice to transport to his basketball outings at a nearby school. This model, like the Supersonic, offered pleasing sound, but it included an even more appealing feature: a big bass boost. Now that piqued his interest! Other features which this model included were programmability, thirty-second anti-skip, and AM/FM radio. Lastly, the Barrett model cost sixty dollars. After the final decision, Jeff could clearly communicate the reasons for his choice. He selected the Blaring Barrett over the Supersonic because of the portability, the price, and the power of the big bass boost.*

20.6 Literary Device

Alliteration is the repetition of sounds in writing.

The repetition of sounds in writing, known as **alliteration**, will be the literary device for this lesson. Even though writing is often read silently, readers have an "internal ear" that delights in proper use of patterns to create interest. When writing prose, one must be careful to avoid overuse of this strategy since doing so can prevent the writing from being taken seriously. This simple tool, though, should be utilized periodically by the accomplished writer. Numerous examples of alliteration fill the paragraphs in 20C and 20D. Here are a few samples:

- *After evaluating a number of features, Jeff selected the Blaring Barrett Boom Box over the Supersonic Square Sound System.*

- *Sound was a second consideration.*

- *He selected the Blaring Barrett because of portability, price, and the power of the big bass boost.*

WEEK 20
Comparison Paragraphs

Daily Assignments

—— Day 1 ——

A. Reading Assignment:
Study the Week 20 Lesson on comparison paragraphs thoroughly.

B. Lesson Exercise:
Answer the following questions in complete sentences:
1. Once a writer has decided what to compare in a comparison paragraph, what is the next step?
2. What are the two development options for a comparison composition?
3. What is alliteration?

C. Writing Exercise:
1. Create a comparison chart like the one on page 124, and use it to brainstorm a comparison paragraph on a topic approved by your instructor. Write your brainstorming list neatly, in a manner that is suitable for submission with your final draft.

    Purpose: inform or persuade
    Audience: peers
    Topic suggestions: two restaurants, two different brands of a product, your city with another city.

2. Do research as needed for supporting information. Gather bibliographic information, general notes on the topic, and prepare quotations, summaries, or paraphrases to offer in support of your position as described in the Week 10 Lesson. You will need at least one source, and no more than two, for this week's paragraph.

3. Write a topic sentence and create a planning outline for this comparison paragraph. The planning outline will also be submitted to your instructor with your final draft.

—— Day 2 ——

A. Style Drill:
Identify the two style points used in the following sentence.

Running down the hill, he chased his hat, which was blowing away in the wind.

B. **Writing Exercise:**
Draft the entire comparison paragraph which you planned on Day 1. Insert proper citations for any research evidence included. This week's literary device, alliteration, is to be included in the paragraph and may be added any time between now and Day 4. If you find it necessary, revise your planning outline and create a new copy for submission. Otherwise, complete this first draft of your paragraph so that you can mark corrections on it tomorrow. This corrected copy will be submitted with your final draft on Day 5.

Day 3

A. **Formality Drill:**
Using the formality and grammar rules explained in Lesson 2, rewrite the sentence below in proper form:

    He put a lot of effort into the run.

B. **Writing Exercise:**
1. *Now begin to edit your paragraph draft from yesterday, marking corrections and changes on your rough draft. Consult the paragraph checklist to insure that you are following set guidelines.*
2. *Add three different style points on this day.*
3. *Create another copy of this revision for submission on Day 5.*

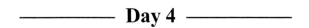

Day 4

A. **Style Drill:**
Identify the style point used in the following sentence.

    Above the clouds thrust majestic Mount Hood.

B. **Writing Exercise:**
1. *Go over your paragraph and correct all spelling, punctuation, and grammatical errors.*
2. *This week's literary device, alliteration, must be added to the paragraph by this day. Again, if you cannot fit the device into the assignment, write two sample sentences, each including this week's literary device, and submit them with your paragraph.*
3. *Make other improvements in words and phrases that may come to mind.*
4. *Prepare a revised draft of your paragraph.*

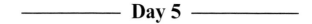

Day 5

A. Formality Drill:

Using the formality and grammar rules explained in Lesson 2, rewrite the sentence below in proper form:

You must consider the situation carefully.

B. Writing Exercise:

1. *The final day to polish your paragraph has come. Read the paragraph aloud slowly and listen for problem areas. Now, have someone else read it to you so that you can listen and be certain that the product is well-written.*

2. *Using the Paragraph Checklist, review your paragraph. Check off each guideline in the upper section when you have verified that you have followed it. In the lower section, mark the style points you have used. On your final draft, identify these style points by writing the corresponding number from the checklist directly above each one, and label the literary device.*

3. *Make certain that the text includes appropriate parenthetical references in text, and that the "Works Cited" page is complete.*

4. *Make certain that the assignment is double-spaced, has one inch margins, has page numbering if needed, and that it includes the proper heading required by your instructor. Along with name and date, the heading should include paragraph type, paragraph purpose, and intended audience.*

5. *Submit your work to the instructor:*
    a. *Final draft paragraph*
    b. *"Works Cited" page, as applicable*
    c. *Literary device, if written separately*
    d. *Paragraph checklist*
    e. *All drafts*
    f. *Topic sentence & planning outline*
    g. *Comparison chart*

WEEK 21
Comparison Paragraphs (continued)

Daily Assignments

Day 1

A. Formality Drill:
Using the formality and grammar rules explained in Lesson 2, rewrite the sentence below in proper form:

When kids will not be quiet during a concert, it really bugs listeners.

B. Writing Exercise:
This week you will prepare for a timed writing of a comparison paragraph on Day 5. To prepare for the paragraph, you will do research and gather bibliographic information, general notes on the topic, and prepare quotations, summaries, or paraphrases to offer in support of your position as described in Week 10. Today, brainstorm possible contentions for your topic sentence. Next, gather the sources needed for your research. Citings from at least one source and a maximum of two sources will be required.

> *Topic: student choice*
> *Purpose: inform or persuade*
> *Audience: student choice based on selected topic*
> *Suggested ideas: two related animals (example: bobcat/housecat), two presidents, two historical figures, two planets, two geographic regions, the U. S. Presidency with a monarchy.*

Day 2

A. Style Drill:
Identify the style point used in the following sentence.

Sweating in the oppressive heat, the family decided to eat dinner in a restaurant which had air conditioning.

B. Writing Exercise:
1. *From a minimum of two sources, take general notes as needed on the topic and obtain at least six quotes, summaries, or paraphrases.*

2. *Develop a list of the bibliographic information which corresponds to your notes. On the day you write your paragraph, you will draw from this list for your "Works Cited" page. Naturally, only the sources you cite in your paragraph will be cited on the "Works Cited" page. General or common knowledge gleaned from your sources need not be specifically cited.*

Day 3

A. Formality Drill:
Using the formality and grammar rules explained in Lesson 2, rewrite the sentence below in proper form:

Can you tell me what the future holds?

B. Writing Exercise:
1. *Complete your research.*
2. *Brainstorm supporting points from your research and your own knowledge about the topic.*
3. *Formulate a final topic sentence and develop a planning outline for your paragraph.*

Day 4

A. Style Drill:
Identify the style point used in the following sentence.

For the sake of her future, she established an even stricter household budget.

B. Writing Exercise:
1. *Of the quotes you compiled, you may use only two in this paragraph. Today, determine which quotes you will use and where they will fit into the planning outline.* <u>You may not pre-write your paragraph.</u>
2. *Create a Working Bibliography for all the sources you studied.* <u>Do not create the "Works Cited" page.</u>
3. *Gather all materials which you will need for tomorrow's timed write:*
    a. *Notes*
    b. *Topic sentence and planning outline*
    c. *Working Bibliography page*
    d. *Brainstorming*

Day 5

A. Grammar Drill:
Review the prepositions list.

B. Formality Drill:
Using the formality and grammar rules explained in Lesson 2, rewrite the sentence below in proper form:

The race car crossed the track with a lurch.

C. Writing Exercise:
Today's exercise will be a 30-minute timed write.

1. *Using your notes and planning outline, write a comparison paragraph on your chosen topic. Be certain to include two parenthetical citations in the paragraph.*

    Audience: student choice based on selected topic
    Purpose: inform or persuade

2. *Develop a "Works Cited" page for your sources. It should be organized according to MLA guidelines. You may refer back to the Week 10 Lesson and to the documentation formats in Appendix D on page 202.*

3. *When the time is up, submit the following to your instructor:*

    a. *Written paragraph*
    b. *"Works Cited" page*
    c. *Working Bibliography page*
    d. *Planning outline*
    e. *Notes, quotations and other source material*

WEEK 22
Comparison Paragraphs (continued)

Daily Assignments

―――― **Day 1** ――――

A. Formality Drill:
Using the formality and grammar rules explained in Lesson 2, rewrite the sentence below in proper form:

She tells her mother how the young people decided to go ice skating after the concert.

B. Writing Exercise:
1. *Based on the guidelines given in Week 12 Lesson, critique the following paragraph, marking scores, comments, and corrections on a grading form copied from Appendix E.*

    Assignment: compare something from the past with the same thing today
    Type of paragraph: comparison
    Purpose: persuade
    Audience: peers

    Communication today is better than that of the early 1900's based on variety, cost, and dependability. In the early 1900's there were only a few forms of communication. The postal service, the telegraph, and the newly developed telephone were the primary options. The mail and telegraph were reasonably inexpensive, and thus affordable for the average person. The new telephone, however, was more expensive, and mostly used by the upper class. These forms of communication were also not very dependable. The mail service was slow, the telegraph lines could be down, and the telephone often had bad reception. In contrast to the past, communication today offers many options. Telephones, cell phones, e-mail, Internet, facsimile (fax), as well as the postal service are the mot commonly used forms of communication today. All of these are fairly inexpensive, and in the case of e-mail and Internet, often free. Also, these forms of communication are very dependable and speedy. Although servers may crash or telephones may be out, overall the modern person can usually depend on any of these types. When looking at communication, past and present, in the light of these three criteria, communication today is definitely superior.

2. *Discuss your evaluation with your instructor.*

―――― **Day 2** ――――

A. Style Drill:
Identify the style point used in the following sentence.

Believing in a representative government, the Founders established a representative republic.

B. Writing Exercise:
Based on your instructor's feedback, you will begin an edit week, reworking the comparison paragraph which you wrote in Week 20. Today, edit all form, structure, and logic problems in the paragraph. This includes points off topic, unsupported contentions, and all other points in the top section of the grading form. If necessary, make a new planning outline and re-write portions which are not correct. Additionally, do more research, as needed, in order to present your points more adequately.

Day 3

A. Formality Drill:
Using the formality and grammar rules explained in Lesson 2, rewrite the sentence below in proper form:

Jack could not decide about the trip because too many things were up in the air.

B. Writing Exercise:
Today, continue editing your comparison paragraph by correcting stylistic and impression problems. This includes sentence variety, emphasis, transitions, and all other parts in the "Impression" portion of the grading form.

Day 4

A. Style Drill:
Identify the style point used in the following sentence.

Surprisingly, both men had been living in the same town for the past ten years, yet they had never seen one another before meeting at the fair.

B. Writing Exercise:
Today, correct any mechanical errors in your paragraph. This includes grammar, spelling, punctuation, and informalities. Also, prepare all items needed with your re-submission, including anything not submitted the first time.

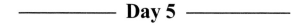

Day 5

A. Grammar Drill:
Review the prepositions.

B. Formality Drill:
Using the formality and grammar rules explained in Lesson 2, rewrite the sentence below in proper form:

The chef carefully grates garlic into the sizzling oil. Then add a pinch of salt.

C. Writing Exercise:
1. Again, read your work aloud and be certain that you have improved in every area which the instructor has deemed necessary. Rewrite a final draft of your paragraph.
2. Submit:
    a. Your rewritten paragraph.
    b. Any other rewritten items – ie. brainstorming, outline, etc.
    c. The evaluation form filled out by your instructor.
    d. The paragraph on which your teacher wrote corrections.
    e. Any items which you did not submit with your first paragraph.

WEEK 23

Lesson: *Cause and Effect Paragraphs*

23.1 Introduction

Cause and effect paragraphs examine what started something or what resulted from something. Besides discussing cause and effect relationships, this paragraph may also speculate the outcomes of a current situation or an anticipated circumstance. The paragraphs of this type assigned in this course will focus on either causes or effects, but not both. To discuss both causes and effects would likely take more than a single paragraph in most cases.

A cause and effect paragraph considers what makes something happen or looks at consequences of something.

23.2 Topic Sentence

Topic sentences in cause and effect paragraphs will establish a contention which may range from speculation to a firm contention. In the following topic sentence, the writer speculates as to possible effects if a situation is not corrected:

> *If the dike is not repaired, damage to the town and surrounding areas <u>could</u> be devastating.*

In other instances, the writer may choose to take a strong position with his contention:

> *If the dike is not repaired, damage to the town and surrounding areas <u>will</u> be devastating.*

The topic sentence may also set the stage to examine a number of causes or effects:

> *Massive flooding in the town was caused by the heavy rainfall, the release of water from the dam, and the failure of the unmaintained dike.*

> *Failure of the dike resulted in the devastation of businesses, the loss of livestock, and the drowning of two Princeton townspeople.*

Since the topic sentence will establish the goal of the paragraph, the writer must spend time carefully considering his approach.

23.3 Paragraph Development

Development of this type of paragraph can follow different patterns. To understand this, it might be helpful to view the cause and effect paragraph as a formula. One such formula might look like this:

> *cause #1 + cause #2 + cause #3 = effect*

A paragraph following this pattern will contend that an effect did, or will, result from certain causes. In developing the paragraph, each cause will need to be discussed and evidence given to show how each cause led to the effect.

Another pattern may be the following:

> *cause = effect #1, #2, #3*

In this pattern, specific effects are contended to result from a cause. The writer will need to discuss each effect and establish its connection to the cause.

Often causes and their effects are more complex. For example, European governments, borders, and relationships were vastly different after World War I than before that time. It would be a shallow treatment of the subject to simply say World War I caused the changes. The truth is that inherent problems in Europe caused World War I and led to change. This subject would likely fill a book, but it serves to point out that there may not be a simple relationship between a cause and an effect. For this example, the formula might look like this:

> cause #1 + cause #2 + cause #3 produced: <u>event</u> resulting in: effect #1, effect #2, effect #3

Care must be taken to ensure that every contention made in the topic sentence is covered within the paragraph. It is easy with this type of paragraph to establish contentions for both causes and effects, thereby creating a topic too broad for one paragraph. For example:

> *The town's failure to maintain the dike resulted in the devastation of businesses, the loss of livestock, and the drowning of two townspeople.*

The above topic sentence establishes contentions about the maintenance of the dike (cause) as well as impact on businesses, livestock, and townspeople (effects). Proving this many contentions will be too much to cover with a single paragraph. Therefore, it would be best to simplify the topic sentence and limit the discussion to only the causes or only the effects:

> *Failure of the dike resulted in the devastation of businesses, the loss of livestock, and the drowning of two Princeton townspeople.*

23.4 Concluding Sentence

The concluding sentence in this type of paragraph will almost always restate the contention for emphasis. However, to avoid boring repetition, a skillful writer will make the restatement using new structure and vocabulary.

<u>Effect Paragraph</u>

Topic sentence: *Failure of the dike resulted in the devastation of businesses, the loss of livestock, and the drowning of two Princeton townspeople.*

Concluding sentence: *Princeton's tragic losses were clearly a consequence of the dike's collapse.*

<u>Speculative Effect Paragraph</u>

Topic sentence: *If the dike is not repaired, damage to the town and surrounding areas could be devastating.*

Concluding sentence: *In order to avoid overwhelming harm to this city, repairs to the dike must be made without delay.*

Optional concluding sentence: *Clearly, one can see the potential for devastating harms to this city if the dike is not repaired.*

23.5 Avoid flawed reasoning

An easy error to make when considering a cause and effect paragraph is the assumption that because one event happened first, it caused another or others. For example, this author trudged heavily down the hall of her home with a huge armload of laundry and dropped it to the floor. Within a few seconds, the Ash Wednesday earthquake of 2000 shook the house, the city, the state, and the state to the north. Does this mean that the huge pile of laundry falling to the floor produced the earthquake? Of course, it does not. Completely different forces bring about earthquakes. It is possible to mistakenly assume that just because one action preceded another, the first is the cause of the second. One must be careful to discern whether a first occurrence is a true cause or just coincidence. Logic teachers refer to this error by a Latin term: **post hoc, ergo propter hoc** ("after this, therefore because of this.").

Post hoc, ergo propter hoc:

"After this, therefore because of this."

The following are examples of cause and effect paragraphs. While the first paragraph resembles a process paragraph, it is considered a cause paragraph in this instance because it details the specific cause of a specific event. The second sample deals with the effects of an event.

23A - Sample Cause Paragraph

The February 2001 Olympia earthquake was caused by release of stress along the Cascadia Subduction Zone. This area lies just off the coast of Oregon and Washington where the North American and Juan de Fuca plates come together. Forces within the earth pressing the two plates together have caused the smaller Juan de Fuca plate to bend and slip under the North American plate, an action referred to as subduction. Over many years, the forces pushing the plates together caused stresses to build up along the adjoining edges of both plates within the subduction zone. Finally, like a stick bent too far, the Juan de Fuca plate cracked on February 28, 2001 as it bent under the pressure of the North American plate. This cracking, centered about ten miles northeast of Olympia and thirty-five miles deep, relieved some of the accumulated stress, but the resulting shock waves created an earthquake felt by people within a several hundred mile radius. The Olympia quake of 2001 has reminded Northwesterners of the danger from the fault lines beneath them.

23B - Sample Effect Paragraph

The year 2000 Pacific Northwest earthquake produced many repercussions. One of the main effects was damage to water and fuel lines, buildings, bridges, and other structures. Along with the damage to utility lines, broken windows, weakened supports, and many other structural damages resulted. Another effect from the earthquake was injuries to inhabitants in areas surrounding the disaster. Fallen roofs, walls, and various dangerous situations caused physical harm to many. This earthquake also created a greater awareness of the need for earthquake preparedness. It helped remind those in the region of the need for storing food and water in preparation for a disaster, as well as earthquake-proofing bridges and other structures. Furthermore, as a result of the earthquake, the government sent aid to the affected areas. Federal disaster agencies gave assistance in cleanup and the distribution of supplies. Lastly, one of the most lingering effects of the earthquake was fear. Many people are fearful of future larger earthquakes and what might result if another does occur. This earthquake brought about numerous lasting effects in the Northwest.

Copyright 2001 Georgia Hill, Used by permission.
Written by Georgia Hill, Beaverton, Oregon.

23.6 Literary Device

The figurative language technique practiced this week is a subcategory of metaphor. Attributing human characteristics or traits to something nonhuman is **personification**. Either an inanimate object or an abstract concept may be endowed with human traits. Strategic placement of this literary device will add richness and clarity to prose writing since it evokes a mental picture in the reader's mind. The following are examples of personification:

Personification is attributing human qualities to an object or concept.

23C - Personification Examples

Verb:	The dark prison cell <u>opened</u> its gaping mouth to <u>swallow</u> the condemned man.
	Thomas Kinkade paintings <u>beckon</u> onlookers to explore their beauty.
	Formal writing <u>requires</u> that the writer adheres to strict standards.
	The terrorist acts of September 11, 2001 <u>demand</u> a response.
Adjective:	The hikers contemplated the <u>threatening</u> sky.
	A <u>mighty</u> oak stood in the middle of the field.
Adverb:	Clothes hung <u>lazily</u> over the line across the porch.
Pronoun:	Grandpa's old tractor had pulled <u>her</u> last plow.
Noun and verb:	The spelunkers felt the <u>grip</u> of the darkness when their lamps <u>died</u>.

WEEK 23
Cause and Effect Paragraphs

Daily Assignments

---— Day 1 ———

A. Reading Assignment:
Study the Week 23 Lesson on cause and effect paragraphs thoroughly.

B. Lesson Exercise:
Answer the following questions with complete sentences:
1. Explain the two simplest development patterns for a cause and effect paragraph.
2. What common flaw in reasoning occurs in cause and effect assignments?
3. What is personification?

C. Writing Exercise:
1. *Brainstorm a cause paragraph or an effect paragraph on a topic approved by your instructor. Write your brainstorming list neatly, in a manner that is suitable for submission with your final draft.*

    Purpose: inform or persuade
    Audience: instructor choice
    Topic suggestions: evaluate the causes or effects of a natural disaster, short term effects of the terrorist attacks on 9/11/01, causes for a student procrastinating doing homework, effects when a student procrastinates homework

2. *Do research as needed for supporting information. You will need at least one source and no more than three sources. You should have no more than three citations for quotes, summaries, or paraphrases in this assignment. Gather bibliographic information, general notes on the topic, and prepare quotations, summaries, or paraphrases to offer in support of your position as described in the Week 10 Lesson.*

3. *Write a topic sentence and create a planning outline for this paragraph. The planning outline will also be submitted to your instructor with your final draft.*

---— Day 2 ———

A. Style Drill:
Identify the style point used in the following sentence.

To open the bottle, the woman finally resorted to using a pipe wrench.

B. **Writing Exercise:**
Draft the entire cause/effect paragraph which you planned on Day 1. Insert proper citations for any research evidence included. This week's literary device, personification, is to be included in the paragraph and may be added any time between now and Day 4. If you find it necessary, revise your planning outline for submission. Otherwise, complete this first draft of your paragraph and create a copy today so that you can mark corrections on it tomorrow. This corrected copy will be submitted with your final draft on Day 5.

Day 3

A. **Formality Drill:**
Using the formality and grammar rules explained in Lesson 2, rewrite the sentence below in proper form:

The young people went bananas over the new sports car.

B. **Writing Exercise:**
1. *Now, begin to edit your paragraph draft from yesterday, marking corrections and changes on your rough draft. Consult the paragraph checklist to insure that you are following set guidelines.*

2. *Add three different style points on this day.*

3. *Create another copy of this revision for submission on Day 5.*

Day 4

A. **Style Drill:**
Identify the style point used in the following sentence.

Her wound, which the doctor stitched closed, developed an infection.

B. **Writing Exercise:**
1. *Go over your paragraph and correct all spelling, punctuation, and grammatical errors.*

2. *This week's literary device must be added to the paragraph by this day. Again, if you cannot fit the device into the assignment, write two sample sentences, each including this week's literary device, and submit them with your paragraph.*

3. *Make other improvements in words and phrases that may come to mind.*

4. *Prepare a revised draft of our paragraph.*

——— Day 5 ———

A. Grammar Drill:
Review the prepositions again today.

B. Formality Drill:
Using the formality and grammar rules explained in Lesson 2, rewrite the sentence below in proper form:

She'll be glad to know that Nicole is back in town.

C. Writing Exercise:
1. *The final day to polish your paragraph has come. Read the paragraph aloud slowly and listen for problem areas. Now, have someone else read it to you so that you can listen and be certain that the product is well-written.*

2. *Using the Paragraph Checklist, review your paragraph. Check off each guideline in the upper section when you have verified that you have followed it. In the lower section, mark the style points you have used. On your final draft, identify these style points by writing the corresponding number from the checklist directly above each one, and label the literary device.*

3. *Make certain that the text includes appropriate parenthetical references in-text, and that the "Works Cited" page is complete.*

4. *Make certain that the assignment is double-spaced, has one inch margins, has page numbering if needed, and that it includes the proper heading required by your instructor. Along with name and date, the heading should include paragraph type, paragraph purpose, and intended audience.*

5. *Submit your work to the instructor:*
   a. *Final draft paragraph*
   b. *"Works Cited" page, as applicable*
   c. *Literary device, if written separately*
   d. *Paragraph checklist*
   e. *All drafts*
   f. *Topic sentence & planning outline*
   g. *Brainstorming*

WEEK 24
Cause and Effect Paragraphs (continued)

Daily Assignments

——————— **Day 1** ———————

A. Formality Drill:
Using the formality and grammar rules explained in Lesson 2, rewrite the sentence below in proper form:

The situation revealed her true colors.

B. Writing Exercise:
This week you will prepare for a timed writing of a cause paragraph or an effect paragraph on Day 5. To prepare for the paragraph, you will do research and gather bibliographic information, general notes on the topic, and prepare quotations, summaries, or paraphrases to offer in support of your position as described in Week 10. Today, brainstorm possible contentions for your topic sentence. Next, gather the sources needed for your research. Citings from at least two sources will be required.

> *Topic: student choice*
> *Purpose: inform or persuade*
> *Audience: student choice*
> *Suggested topic: What causes high numbers of forest fires? What causes young people to drive recklessly?*

——————— **Day 2** ———————

A. Style Drill:
Identify the style point used in the following sentence.

Into the bucket of honey reached Winnie the Pooh.

B. Writing Exercise:
1. *From a minimum of two sources, take general notes as needed on the topic and obtain at least six quotes, summaries, or paraphrases.*

2. *Develop a list of the bibliographic information which corresponds to your notes. On the day you write your paragraph, you will draw from this list for your "Works Cited" page. Naturally, only the sources you cite in your paragraph will be cited on the "Works Cited" page. General or common knowledge gleaned from your sources need not be specifically cited.*

Put That In Writing 145

──────── **Day 3** ────────

A. Formality Drill:
Using the formality and grammar rules explained in Lesson 2, rewrite the sentence below in proper form:

You should have seen her face when I told her the news that she was the first place winner.

B. Writing Exercise:
1. *Complete your research.*
2. *Brainstorm supporting points from your research and your own knowledge about the topic.*
3. *Formulate a final topic sentence and develop a planning outline for your paragraph.*

──────── **Day 4** ────────

A. Style Drill:
Identify the style point used in the following sentence.

Laughing, Ashley enticed the cat to play with the string.

B. Writing Exercise:
1. *Of the quotes you compiled, you may use only two in this paragraph. Today, determine which quotes you will use and where they will fit into the planning outline.* <u>You may not pre-write your paragraph.</u>
2. *Create a Working Bibliography for all the sources you studied.* <u>Do not create the "Works Cited" page.</u>
3. *Gather all materials which you will need for tomorrow's timed write:*
    a. *Note cards*
    b. *Topic sentence and planning outline*
    c. *Working Bibliography page*
    d. *Brainstorming*

──────── **Day 5** ────────

A. Formality Drill:
Using the formality and grammar rules explained in Lesson 2, rewrite the sentence below in proper form:

Soap is the item she went to the store for.

B. Writing Exercise:

Today's exercise will be a 30-minute timed write.

1. Using your notes and planning outline, write a cause paragraph or effect paragraph on your chosen topic. Be certain to include two parenthetical references in the paragraph.

2. Develop a "Works Cited" page for your sources. It should be organized according to MLA guidelines. You may refer back to the Week 10 Lesson and to the documentation formats in Appendix D on page 202.

3. When the time is up, submit the following to your instructor:
    a. Written paragraph
    b. "Works Cited" page
    c. Working Bibliography page
    d. Planning outline
    e. Brainstorming
    f. Note cards

WEEK 25
Cause and Effect Paragraphs (continued)

Daily Assignments

— Day 1 —

A. Formality Drill:
Using the formality and grammar rules explained in Lesson 2, rewrite the sentence below in proper form:

The pencil was sharpened down to the eraser.

B. Writing Exercise:
1. *Based on the guidelines given in Week 12 Lesson, critique the following paragraph, marking scores, comments, and corrections on a grading form copied from Appendix E.*

   Assignment: student choice of topic
   Type of paragraph: cause or effect
   Purpose: persuade
   Audience: peers

   A number of character enhancements may be obtained by participating in chess. First, one experiences improvements in mental abilities. Training one's mind to see positions in the future and forecast the opponent's moves can boost the ability to think logically. Calculating whether or not a position is a prediction of winning also heightens a chess player's ability to think. There is also much discipline to be gained by playing chess. Sitting through six-hour games trains a player to maintain a high level of concentration. At competitions, strict regulations — about maintaining a silent atmosphere, playing within the rules, shaking hands with the opponent, and wishing him well — help develop an attitude of sportsmanship. When cramped in a room with forty other people doing almost exactly the same thing, it is hard not to meet someone new, or at least socialize. Another easy way to get to know other chess players is by joining a chess club, where one can meet many other chess "buddies." Many of these skills can be of benefit in one's practical, everyday decisions.

2. *Discuss your evaluation with your instructor.*

— Day 2 —

A. Style Drill:
Identify the style point used in the following sentence.

When the snow gets deep enough, Olivia will build a huge snowman.

B. Writing Exercise:
Based on your instructor's feedback, you will begin an edit week, reworking the cause or effect paragraph which you wrote in Week 23. Today, edit all form, structure, and logic

problems in the paragraph. This includes points off topic, unsupported contentions, and all other points in the top section of grading form. If necessary, make a new planning outline and rewrite portions which are not correct. Additionally, do more research as needed in order to present your points more adequately.

Day 3

A. Formality Drill:
Using the formality and grammar rules explained in Lesson 2, rewrite the sentence below in proper form:

Joel couldn't run the race without his special shoes.

B. Writing Exercise:
Today, continue editing your cause/effect paragraph by correcting stylistic and impression problems. This includes sentence variety, emphasis, transitions, and all other parts in the "Impression" portion of the grading form.

Day 4

A. Style Drill:
Identify the style point used in the following sentence.

To prepare for the marathon, Josiah ran several miles every day.

B. Writing Exercise:
Today, correct any mechanical errors in your paragraph. This includes grammar, spelling, punctuation, and informalities. Also, prepare all items needed with your re-submission, including anything not submitted the first time.

Day 5

A. Grammar Drill:
Review the prepositions again today.

B. Formality Drill:
Using the formality and grammar rules explained in Lesson 2, rewrite the sentence below in proper form:

Sumptuous meals were prepared by the chef.

C. Writing Exercise:
1. *Again, read your work aloud and be certain that you have improved in every area which the instructor has deemed necessary. Rewrite a final draft of your paragraph.*

2. Submit:
    a. Your rewritten paragraph.
    b. Any other rewritten items – ie. brainstorming, outline, etc.
    c. The evaluation form filled out by your instructor.
    d. The paragraph on which your teacher wrote corrections.
    e. Any items which you did not submit with your first paragraph.

D. Test:
Complete Week 25 Quiz over Week 20 and Week 23 Lessons.

WEEK 26

Lesson: *Analogy Paragraphs*

26.1 Introduction

An **analogy** explains one item or concept using attributes of another. At first glance this may seem to be the same as a simile or metaphor; however, an analogy extends the association much further by drawing more than one parallel. In an essay, the analogy will usually be only a small part, comprising just a few sentences in a paragraph, or at most, a whole paragraph. It will be presented along with other supporting evidence for some of the following reasons:

1. To simplify something complicated
2. To familiarize the reader with something new
3. To create a mental picture
4. To add interest
5. To make the concept easier for the reader to retain

Since an analogy, like the simile and metaphor, also compares items of different classes not normally associated, this writing strategy sparks the reader's curiosity and imagination.

An analogy paragraph explains one item or concept using attributes of another.

26.2 Planning

Planning an analogy is much like planning a comparison paragraph. The writer should first brainstorm the attributes of the topic being explained. Next, he must decide what to compare with the topic and brainstorm possible similarities. Several points of likeness are required for the association to qualify as an analogy. Drawing only a couple of points of comparison will not do; three or more parallels are a must. For example, one might consider the possibility of connecting life as a youngest child to life as a lowly army private. A brainstorming list of parallels might look something like the list in Illustration 26A. From this list, a paragraph such as the one in Illustration 26B could be written.

26A - Sample Brainstorming for Analogy

Home	Military Base
• *parents*	• *commanders*
• *older siblings*	• *sergeants*
• *chores*	• *duties*
• *always receiving instructions*	• *always taking orders*
• *manipulated by those above him*	• *manipulated by those above him*
• *not listened to like other children*	• *not listened to like others above him*
• *pleading ineffective*	• *pleading ineffective*
• *others receive best food*	• *officers receive best food*
• *will always remain the youngest child*	• *a private never receiving promotion*

26B - Sample Analogy Paragraph

> *An anonymous youngest child claims that being the youngest in the family is like living on a military base where he is the only private, and everyone else is an officer. They always seem to receive the best food while he must eat whatever is left. Everywhere he turns, he is taking orders from someone. Daily, the duties of others are delegated down the "ranks" to him. When his chores are compared with his "superiors'," his seem to be more mundane and less critical to the family's "marching orders." Even when he has a moment to himself, someone comes into the room and issues new orders. In fact, "sergeants" just above him often order him to deliver, or even trick him into delivering, their requests to the two "commanding officers." As the youngest, it seems that he is not listened to as much as those above him. Superiors ignore the fact that he is picked on by other "soldiers" despite his pleadings, protests, and pain. Finally, his greatest challenge is that he will never rise through the ranks since no matter how old he gets, others will still "pull rank." Like a private who never receives a promotion, he will always be given fewer responsibilities and will always be perceived as less mature. This anonymous "soldier" wonders if it might be possible to have a family without ever having a youngest child.*

26.3 Paragraph development

Development of an analogy paragraph has both similarities and differences with other paragraphs. To follow proper form, the paragraph will begin with a topic sentence. In this case, however, the topic sentence is often written as a simile or metaphor in order to lay the basis for the analogy. Notice the simile in the topic sentence of the above sample:

> *An anonymous youngest child claims that being the youngest in the family <u>is like</u> living on a military base where he is the only private, and everyone else is an officer.*

The analogy then proceeds with a discussion of each comparison point in terms of the object to which the subject is being compared. This is the key to creating an analogy. One does not discuss each attribute and say that it is like an attribute of the other item. Instead, the attributes of the subject are described in terms of the attributes of the object of comparison. Direct similes should be kept to a minimum. The following sentences from the example paragraph above show how the attributes of the youngest child are described in military terms:

> *Everywhere he turns, he is taking <u>orders</u> from someone.*

> *Daily, the <u>duties</u> of others are <u>delegated down the "ranks"</u> to him.*

> *In fact, "<u>sergeants</u>" just above him often <u>order him</u> to deliver, or even trick him into delivering, their requests to the two "<u>commanding officers</u>."*

> *Finally, his greatest challenge is that he will never "<u>rise through the ranks</u>" since no matter how old he gets, others will still "<u>pull rank</u>."*

The topic sentence of an analogy paragraph is usually a simile.

Because the topic sentence has prepared the reader to compare being a youngest child to being a private in the military, the use of military terms throughout the paragraph will cause the reader to draw other military comparisons. He will see that the instructions are like military "orders" even though the writer has not directly said so. He will see that older children seem as though they have a higher "rank," and parents seem like "commanding officers," although the comparisons are not stated in so many words. This is how a strong analogy works, and should be the goal when writing an analogy paragraph.

Finally, an analogy paragraph generally requires a different kind of concluding sentence. Because the entire paragraph works to make a single point, a summary sentence will most likely seem too repetitive. Therefore, the conclusion may simply draw the reader's attention back to the main subject by taking a humorous twist, offering a rhetorical question, or some other unique conclusion.

26.4 Weaknesses of the Analogy

While an analogy can seem to be a perfect way to explain concepts, it does present a few problems. The most glaring issue is that an analogy always breaks down at some point. That is, the parallels are not exact and do not extend over all attributes of the objects. The second difficulty is that the parallels drawn between two objects or ideas must be significant. An analogy is said to "not hold" if it is based on obscure similarities overshadowed by major dissimilarities. Because of these problems, the analogy is the weakest form of proof in support of a contention. Its primary value is in provoking thought.

Problems with analogies:

1. **They break down.**
2. **The parallels must be significant.**

WEEK 26
Analogy Paragraphs

Daily Assignments

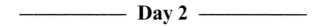

Day 1

A. Reading Assignment:
Study the Week 26 Lesson on analogy paragraphs thoroughly.

B. Lesson Exercise:
Answer the following questions in complete sentences:

1. How is an analogy different from a simile or metaphor?
2. In what form is the topic sentence of an analogy paragraph usually written?
3. How is the subject described throughout an analogy paragraph?
4. Explain two of the problems with analogies.

C. Writing Exercise:

1. *Brainstorm a topic for an analogy. Create a planner like the one on page 151 and <u>fully</u> develop the parallels between the two items being compared. You will submit this planner on Day 5 with your final draft. If needed, do research. No specific number of sources is required, unless your instructor specifies, but be certain to cite any that you use.*

    Purpose: inform
    Audience: peers
    Topic suggestions: raising children/growing a garden, life/sport

2. *Write a topic sentence and create a planning outline for this paragraph. The planning outline will also be submitted to your instructor with your final draft.*

Day 2

A. Style Drill:
Identify the style point used in the following sentence.

   Dr. Ellsworth, who treated Sarah and her sister, quickly understood the situation.

B. Writing Exercise:
Draft the entire analogy paragraph which you planned on Day 1. This week's **literary device is the analogy comprising this paragraph.** *If you find it necessary, revise your planning outline and create a new copy for submission. Otherwise, complete this first draft of your paragraph, so that you can mark corrections on it tomorrow. This corrected copy will be submitted with your final draft on Day 5.*

Day 3

A. Formality Drill:
Using the formality and grammar rules explained in Lesson 2, rewrite the sentence below in proper form:

John's helicopter ride into the Grand Canyon was way cool.

B. Writing Exercise:
1. *Now, begin to edit your paragraph draft from yesterday, marking corrections and changes on your rough draft. Consult the paragraph checklist to insure that you are following set guidelines.*
2. *Add three different style points on this day.*
3. *Create another copy of this revision for submission on Day 5.*

Day 4

A. Style Drill:
Identify the style point used in the following sentence.

When Michael reached the shore, he finally quit rowing.

B. Writing Exercise:
1. *Go over your paragraph and correct all spelling, punctuation, and grammatical errors.*
2. *The analogy, created in your paragraph, serves as this week's literary device. You will not receive a separate score for literary device this week.*
3. *Make other improvements in words and phrases that may come to mind.*
4. *Prepare a revised draft of your paragraph.*

Day 5

A. Grammar Drill:
Rehearse the prepositions again today.

B. Formality Drill:
Using the formality and grammar rules explained in Lesson 2, rewrite the sentence below in proper form:

Abe Lincoln purposed to keep the Union together.

C. Writing Exercise:

1. *The final day to polish your paragraph has come. Read the paragraph aloud slowly and listen for problem areas. Now, have someone else read it to you so that you can listen and be certain that the product is well-written.*

2. *Using the Paragraph Checklist, review your paragraph. Check off each guideline in the upper section when you have verified that you have followed it. In the lower section, mark the style points you have used. On your final draft, identify these style points by writing the corresponding number from the checklist directly above each one.*

3. *Make certain that the assignment is formatted properly.*

4. *Submit your work to the instructor:*
    a. *Final draft paragraph*
    b. *Paragraph checklist*
    c. *All drafts*
    d. *Topic sentence & planning outline*
    e. *Planning chart*
    f. *Brainstorming*

WEEK 27
Analogy Paragraphs (continued)

Daily Assignments

─────── **Day 1** ───────

A. Formality Drill:
Using the formality and grammar rules explained in Lesson 2, rewrite the sentence below in proper form:

It appears that her goose is cooked since civil authorities are filing charges.

B. Writing Exercise:
This week you will prepare for a timed writing of an analogy paragraph on Day 5. To prepare for the paragraph, you will brainstorm comparisons as demonstrated in the lesson. Create a planner like the one on page 151 and <u>fully</u> develop the parallels between the two items being compared. You will submit this planner on Day 5 with your final draft. If needed, do research. Today, brainstorm possible contentions for your topic sentence. No specific number of sources is required, unless your instructor specifies, but be certain to cite any that you use.

Topic: student choice
Purpose: inform or persuade
Audience: peers
Suggested topics: character development/landscaping, blood vessels/highways, other analogy in area of science

─────── **Day 2** ───────

A. Style Drill:
Identify the style point used in the following sentence.

Crushed, he gave up the effort to run again for office.

B. Writing Exercise:
Today, see if you can add any additional ideas to yesterday's development chart. Then determine which parallels will best fit into your paragraph.

─────── **Day 3** ───────

A. Formality Drill:
Using the formality and grammar rules explained in Lesson 2, rewrite the sentence below in proper form:

An innovative computer software was installed by the network administrator.

B. **Writing Exercise:**
1. Complete any research.
2. Formulate a final topic sentence and write the points on your planner into a logical planning outline for submission with your work on Day 5.
3. Begin a planning outline for your analogy paragraph.

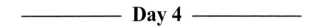
Day 4

A. **Style Drill:**
Identify the style point used in the following sentence.

The dog, which had earlier been shut up in the house, loved tromping around on the roof.

B. **Writing Exercise:**
1. Review your planning outline, making certain that your ideas will work and that they are your own. Outside sources should only work to support your points. <u>You may not pre-write your paragraph</u>.
2. Gather all materials which you will need for tomorrow's timed write:
    a. Working Bibliography and note cards (if outside sources are used)
    b. Topic sentence and planning outline
    c. Brainstorming

Day 5

A. **Formality Drill:**
Using the formality and grammar rules explained in Lesson 2, rewrite the sentence below in proper form:

Amanda is walking down the street when she decided to stop by her neighbor's house.

B. **Writing Exercise:**
Today's exercise will be a 30-minute timed write.

1. Using your notes and planning outline, write an analogy paragraph on your chosen topic. Be certain to include parenthetical citations if you include specific information from sources.
2. Develop a "Works Cited" page for your sources. It should be organized according to MLA guidelines. You may refer back to the Week 10 Lesson and to the documentation formats in Appendix D on page 202. When the time is up, submit the following to your instructor:

    a. Written paragraph
    b. "Works Cited" page
    c. Working Bibliography page
    d. Planning outline
    e. Planning chart
    f. Brainstorming
    g. Note cards

WEEK 28
Analogy Paragraphs (continued)

Daily Assignments

——————— **Day 1** ———————

A. Formality Drill:
Using the formality and grammar rules explained in Lesson 2, rewrite the sentence below in proper form:

As Ashley and Olivia told their hilarious story, she laughed until she cried.

B. Writing Exercise:

1. *Based on the guidelines given in Week 12 Lesson, critique the following paragraph, marking scores, comments, and corrections on a grading form copied from Appendix E.*

   Assignment: student choice of topic
   Type of paragraph: analogy
   Purpose: persuade
   Audience: parents

       Like a day at the circus was the poor mother's day with her children. As the "show" of the day began, she worked to get everyone into their proper "rings." With each child doin his chores, it seemed that all was running smoothly. However, the real tricks began when she received the first phone call from a friend in distress. While she was tethered to the phone, her children began to jump off the couch and somersault across the living room floor. Like flying trapeze artists, they swung up and down the railing along the stairs. With a quick change of clothes, circus employees move from routine to routine. In the same manner, her children changed clothes and began to involve the pets in their raucous tricks. The dog was made to walk on the window sill while the cat, dressed in a too-too, was made to dance by dangling a string in front of her. Like clowns desperate for attention, her children stuffed the cat into a doll stroller and pushed it around the room. Finally, the phone call ended and the mother knew it was time for her to play the role of lion tamer and bring the animals into submission. Control was established until neighborhood children came to play after school. Like a man shot from a cannon, the second son launched himself off the trampoline, breaking his arm. The circus ended on a somber note as the family drove home from the doctor with one child in a cast. Hoping for a quieter day tomorrow, the mother tucked all her clowns into bed. Thankfully, she reasoned, not every day is like this.

2. Discuss that evaluation with your instructor.

——————— **Day 2** ———————

A. Style Drill:
Identify the style point used in the following sentence.

For his mother, Jeff ordered a special compact disc.

B. Writing Exercise:
Based on your instructor's feedback, you will begin an edit week, reworking the analogy paragraph which you wrote in Week 26. Today, edit all form, structure, and logic problems in the paragraph. This includes points off topic, unsupported contentions, and all other points in the top section of grading form. If necessary, make a new planning outline and rewrite portions which are not correct. Additionally, do more research as needed in order to present your points more adequately.

Day 3

A. Formality Drill:
Using the formality and grammar rules explained in Lesson 2, rewrite the sentence below in proper form:

Elysse couldn't wait to finish her job, so she and Mercy would have opportunity to cool off in the water fountain.

B. Writing Exercise:
Today, continue editing your cause or effect paragraph by correcting stylistic and impression problems. This includes sentence variety, emphasis, transitions, and all other parts in the "Impression" portion of grading form.

Day 4

A. Style Drill:
Identify the style point used in the following sentence.

While he was in hiding from the Pope, Martin Luther kept himself extremely busy translating the Bible.

B. Writing Exercise:
Today, correct any mechanical errors in your paragraph. This includes grammar, spelling, punctuation, and informalities. Also, prepare all items needed with your re-submission, including anything not submitted the first time.

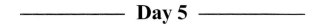

Day 5

A. Grammar Drill:
Review the prepositions again today.

B. Formality Drill:
Using the formality and grammar rules explained in Lesson 2, rewrite the sentence below in proper form:

Georgian turned off the fan with a click.

C. Writing Exercise:
1. *Again, read your work aloud and be certain that you have improved in every area which the instructor has deemed necessary. Rewrite a final draft of your paragraph.*
2. *Submit:*
    a. *Your rewritten paragraph.*
    b. *Any other rewritten items – ie. brainstorming, outline, etc.*
    c. *The evaluation form filled out by your instructor.*
    d. *The paragraph on which your teacher wrote corrections.*
    e. *Any items which you did not submit with your first paragraph.*

WEEK 29

Lesson: *Defending a Position*

29.1 Introduction

Any paragraph can, and to some extent does, defend a position. This fact can be clearly demonstrated by looking at some topic sentences of sample paragraphs in previous lessons:

29A - Examples of Positions in Topic Sentences

Type of Paragraph	Topic Sentence	Position to Defend
Descriptive:	Amanda likes her room because it is pleasant to be there.	Amanda's room is pleasant, so she likes it.
Definition:	Understanding the meaning of "humility" helps one see that this trait should be practiced.	Understanding leads one to believe humility is to be practiced.
Narrative:	Fishing at Horning's Hideout proved to be an enjoyable outing for Jeff and his family.	The outing was enjoyable for all.
Process:	Using a telephone calling card is a simple process.	The process is simple.
Cause:	The February 2001 Seattle earthquake was caused by changes beneath the earth's surface.	Changes underground produced the earthquake.
Effect:	The recent Northwest earthquake resulted in many repercussions.	The effects of the earthquake were many.

Experienced writers do not consider the "type" of paragraph they are writing. Rather, they determine the purpose and then use the techniques of description, narration, cause or effect analysis, and so forth, often in combination, to accomplish the purpose. In this lesson, the student will proceed to a more advanced level of writing which does not involve a specific paragraph type, but which might actually be a combination of any of the types of paragraphs studied thus far. The object at this level will be to take a position on a topic and then prove or defend it. In doing so, the student will be required to use the various techniques learned in writing different types of paragraphs.

> *The position paragraph presents logical argument which enables the audience to understand the reasoning of one who holds that position.*

29.2 Purpose

Before dealing with the development of a **"defending a position" paragraph**, its purpose should be considered. The goal of such a paragraph is not necessarily to make one side seem right or wrong. Yes, there are absolute truths, but the goal is to present logical argument which enables the audience to understand the reasoning of one who holds a particular position. The purpose, therefore, is to equip the audience to better reason for themselves regarding the truth.

Sometimes a student will be required to articulate a position which he or she does not hold. For instance, the student may be assigned to write a paragraph defending the position "Dogs are very useful to man" when it may be that the student does not care for dogs and even might prefer cats. The job of the student in such cases will be to set aside personal bias and articulate the position of one who sees dogs as very useful. Knowing how to create this type of paragraph will be very helpful in these instances.

29.3 Topic Sentence

When writing a paragraph which defends a position, the topic sentence will likely be a simple statement of the writer's contention. The student will recall that a contention is a statement or point which one intends to defend. A topic sentence for this paragraph may or may not detail the supporting points. The following two examples demonstrate the difference:

Simple contention:	*Dogs' versatile skills make them very useful to man.*
Contention with detailed points:	*Dogs' able assistance — as police dogs, guide dogs, and search dogs — demonstrates their usefulness to man.*

29.4 Content

In order to defend any position, sufficient evidence must be offered to prove the position. Where does a student find such evidence? It may be that he or she has some knowledge of the topic; however, *students may consider themselves experts on any topic*. They will have to rely on evidence from others in order to support their points. Supporting evidence will fall into categories called **standard logical proofs**. These include:

1. An appeal to some authority on the topic;
2. The use of statistics or facts to support the point;
3. The citation of examples which demonstrate the point;
4. An analysis of the position in order to help the reader gain understanding;
5. Examples from the writer's personal experience;
6. The contradiction of anticipated opposing arguments.

> *Logical proofs:*
> 1. *Authority*
> 2. *Statistics/facts*
> 3. *Example*
> 4. *Analysis*
> 5. *Personal experience*
> 6. *Counter opposition*

Only in lengthy writings will one see all the above proofs utilized. In paragraphs and essays, the number and combination of proofs will vary depending on topic, audience, assignment limits, and degree of persuasion employed. Naturally, all evidence outside the writer's personal experience must be documented according to the guidelines taught in Week 10.

29.5 Concluding Sentence

A standard summary sentence may be fine. However, since persuasion is likely the goal, the writer could offer an appeal or challenge to the reader.

> Summation: *Assisting police, helping the blind, and searching for the missing are ways in which dogs help mankind.*
>
> Appeal: *Assisting police, helping the blind, and searching for the missing are ways in which dogs help mankind. What would we do without them?*

29.6 Problems to avoid

A couple of common errors generally made by students can be easily avoided when writing the persuasive paragraph. The first mistake involves allowing personal passion to overtake reasoned presentation such that the writing dwells too long on one point. Often, this happens in areas where the student holds strict moral standards, thus feeling intensely about the position being expressed. An example of a situation where this problem might occur is when writing a paper about the devaluing of life in our culture. The student may offer abortion as evidence, at which point, the paper may inadvertently become a paper about abortion rather than the topic of devaluation of life in this culture. Yes, the tragedy of abortion certainly serves as evidence of declining values, but other issues such as euthanasia, the murder rate, and the use of fetuses for harvesting stem cells also demonstrate the problem. "Ranting and raving" on one point will lead the emphasis away from the main topic. In order to produce a well-developed argument, all points must receive balanced treatment and be connected to the topic.

A second common error is writing **unsupported contentions**. The student will recall that an unsupported contention is a statement or point which is offered as fact without any supporting evidence to prove it true. One can even produce **under-supported contentions**, for which there is plainly not enough proof to demonstrate the writer's point. Solving this error requires full development and discussion of each point. Each time a contention is made, whether it is the main point, a supporting point, or a supporting detail, a writer must answer the question "How is this true?" by tying the contention to a logical proof. In other words, solid evidence must support it. A thorough planning outline is the first step in this process. At this level, the student can make certain that each key point has supporting information under it. As a second strategy, the writer must carefully read his work and ask himself if any of the sentences in his paper leave the audience with unanswered questions due to a "leap of logic," insufficient information, or failure to explain how the information supports the contention.

An unsupported contention is a statement or point offered as fact without supporting evidence to prove it true.

An under-supported contention results from an under-developed point.

A rhetorical question is one to which the answer is self-evident from the context.

29.7 Literary Device

The **rhetorical question** will be the literary device for this lesson. This can be defined as a question to which the answer is self-evident from the context. It is asked as a technique for engaging the reader rather than to elicit an actual reply. The purpose is to invite the reader to ponder the topic with the writer. Rhetorical questions also make effective transitions, moving the reader along to consideration of the next point. The following sample paragraph ends with a rhetorical question.

29B - Sample Defending a Position Paragraph

Dogs' able assistance — as police dogs, guide dogs, and search dogs — demonstrates their usefulness to man. Law enforcement officers around the world have come to rely on the assistance of trained "K-9's." By trailing a fleeing suspect or searching for a lost person, the dog significantly assists the human officer. In addition to tracking, a canine "cop" will charge a suspect and knock him to the ground so that officers may apprehend the fugitive. Service from the canine officer also extends to searching for drugs and explosives, or even needed evidence. These useful "pets" work equally as well in more people-oriented settings. They have been of service in hostage situations. They have been useful in areas where police are managing unruly crowds. They even shine as community relations representatives, reaching all ages of citizens who might otherwise feel uncomfortable around police officers. Clearly, police dogs have become a critical aid to peace officers around the world (Police Dog). Another area in which "man's best friend" offers service is working as a guide dog. Often, "specially bred Labrador Retrievers, German Shepherds, and Golden Retrievers," help the visually impaired with numerous tasks (Guiding Eyes). Guide dogs walk at a consistent speed to the left and barely forward of their masters. Amazingly, their helpfulness extends to stopping at all curbs and at the bottom and top of all stairs until told to proceed, and they even escort their handlers to elevator buttons. Since they are so focused on their support of their masters, they ignore distractions and readily obey verbal commands (Guide Dog). What freedom these amazing assistants have brought to the visually impaired! Finally, search and rescue dogs offer another kind of support to mankind. These dogs are taught "to find missing people by following scent which is carried on the air" (Search Dogs). No pieces of clothing or effects of the missing person are necessary, and canines can be dispatched quickly while additional search strategies are being planned. Working equally as well in the dark as in daylight, they can help searchers by catching the odor of a human being at approximately 500 meters (Search Dogs). Search dogs have responded to mountain rescues, missing persons, airplane disasters, and even to the rubble of the World Trade Center. Assisting police, helping the blind, and searching for the missing are ways in which dogs help mankind. What would we do without them?

Works Cited

"Police Dog Services." *Royal Canadian Mounted Police.* Internet. (3-14-2002). Available: <www.rcmp-grc.gc.ca/html/dogs.htm>. March 17, 2002.

"The Guiding Eyes." *Guiding Eyes for the Blind, Inc.* Internet. Available: <www.guiding-eyes.org/info/guidinfo.html>. March 17, 2002.

"What a Guide Dog Does." *The Puppy Place.* Internet. Available: <http://thepuppyplace.org>. March 17, 2002.

"What Do Search Dogs Do?" *Search and Rescue Dog Association.* Internet. Available: <www.nsarda.org.uk/what_dp.shtml>. March 17, 2002.

WEEK 29
Defending a Position

Daily Assignments

Day 1

A. Reading Assignment:
Study the Week 29 Lesson on defending a position thoroughly.

B. Lesson Exercise:
Answer the following questions in complete sentences:
1. What is the goal of a "defending a position" paragraph?
2. The types of supporting evidence in a position paragraph are called what?
3. What two problems are to be avoided in a position paragraph?
4. What is a rhetorical question?

C. Writing Exercise:
1. *Brainstorm a possible topic and choose a possible position to defend. Begin researching your topic. You should use a minimum of two and a maximum of three sources. Be certain to gather necessary bibliographic information and take research notes as you work.*

    Purpose: persuade
    Audience: student choice
    Topic suggestions: political or moral issue, solution to a problem, usefulness of a product

2. *Based on today's research, brainstorm possible supporting points for your position. Research these points adequately, writing down research notes and bibliographic information.*

3. *Prepare your brainstorming list in a manner suitable for submission with your final draft.*

Day 2

A. Style Drill:
Identify the style point used in the following sentence.

Running for the train, the family reached the platform just in time to catch a ride.

B. Writing Exercise:
1. *Continue researching your topic. Decide what logical proofs you will use in your paragraph and gather appropriate information for them.*

2. Using the information you have gathered, create a planning outline and write a final topic sentence for a paragraph defending your position.

3. On your outline, identify the logical proofs you are using. For instance, after listing a supporting detail citing numerical data, you would write "statistic" to indicate the kind of logical proof.

4. Write a planning outline for submission with your final draft.

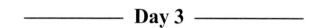

Day 3

A. Formality Drill:
Using the formality and grammar rules explained in Lesson 2, rewrite the sentence below in proper form:

The situation may be difficult, but don't sweat it.

B. Writing Exercise:
Draft the entire paragraph which you planned on Day 2. Remember to incorporate style points and logical proofs. This week's literary device, rhetorical question, is to be included in the paragraph and may be added any time on Day 3 or Day 4. If you find it necessary, revise your planning outline and print a new copy for submission. Otherwise, complete this first draft of your paragraph so that you can mark corrections on it tomorrow. This corrected copy will be submitted with your final draft on Day 5.

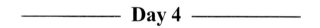

Day 4

A. Style Drill:
Identify the style point used in the following sentence.

Quickly, the driver of the vehicle swerved to avoid the collision.

B. Writing Exercise:
1. Go over your paragraph and correct all spelling, punctuation, and grammatical errors.

2. This week's literary device, the rhetorical question, must be added to the paragraph by this day. It cannot be written separately.

3. Make other improvements in words and phrases that may come to mind.

4. Prepare a revised draft of your paragraph.

Day 5

A. Grammar Drill:
Rehearse the prepositions again today.

B. Formality Drill:
Using the formality and grammar rules explained in Lesson 2, rewrite the sentence below in proper form:

She was obviously having a bad hair day.

C. Writing Exercise:
1. *The final day to polish your paragraph has come. Go over your paragraph and correct all spelling, punctuation, and grammatical errors.*

2. *Read the paragraph aloud slowly and listen for problem areas. Make needed improvements in words and phrases that may come to mind. Now, have someone else read it to you so that you can listen and be certain that the product is well-written.*

3. *Using the paragraph checklist, review your paragraph to be certain that you have followed the guidelines in the upper section. On your final draft, identify these style points by writing the corresponding number from the checklist directly above each style point.*

4. *Make certain that the text includes appropriate parenthetical references in-text and that the "Works Cited" page and "Works Consulted" page, if required, are complete.*

5. *Make certain that the assignment is double-spaced, has one inch margins, has page numbering if needed, and that it includes the proper heading required by your instructor. Create a final copy for submission.*

6. *Submit your work to the instructor:*
   a. *Final paragraph draft*
   b. *"Works Cited" page*
   c. *Literary device, only acceptable in paragraph this week*
   d. *Paragraph checklist*
   e. *All drafts*
   f. *Topic sentence & planning outline*
   g. *Brainstorming*

WEEK 30
Defending a Position (continued)

Daily Assignments

―――――― **Day 1** ――――――

A. Writing Exercise:
This week you will prepare for a timed writing of a paragraph defending a position on Day 5. To prepare for the paragraph, you will do research and gather bibliographic information, general notes on the topic, and prepare quotations, summaries, or paraphrases to offer in support of your position as described in Week 10. Today, brainstorm possible topics for your paragraph. Next, begin your research, making certain to gather necessary bibliographic information and take research notes as you work. Citations from at least two sources will be required.

Topic: student choice
Purpose: persuade
Audience: student choice
Suggested topics*: America's response to the terrorist attack on 9/11/01 was (or was not) correct, nutritional supplements are (or are not) beneficial, cell phone use in automobiles should (or should not) be banned

* *The scope of some of these topics will need to be limited in order to fit a single paragraph.*

―――――― **Day 2** ――――――

A. Writing Exercise:
1. Continue to research your topic. Obtain at least six quotes, summaries, or paraphrases from a minimum of two sources. Decide what logical proofs you will use in your paragraph and gather appropriate information.

2. Continue developing a list of the bibliographic information which corresponds to your notes. On the day you write your paragraph, you will draw from this list for your "Works Cited" page. Naturally, only the sources you use in your paragraph will be cited on the "Works Cited" page. General or common knowledge gleaned from your sources need not be specifically cited.

―――――― **Day 3** ――――――

A. Writing Exercise:
1. Complete your research.

2. Brainstorm supporting points from your research and your own knowledge about the topic.

3. Formulate a final topic sentence and develop a planning outline for your paragraph. Just as you did in Week 29, identify on your outline the logical proofs you will be using.

Day 4

A. Writing Exercise:
1. Of the quotes you compiled, you may use two to three in this paragraph. The remainder of the paragraph must be your own work. Your use of the outside material should work to support the contention stated by your topic sentence. Today, determine which quotes you will use and complete your planning outline. <u>You may not pre-write your paragraph.</u>

2. Create a Working Bibliography for all the sources you studied. <u>Do not create the "Works Cited" page.</u>

3. Gather all materials which you will need for tomorrow's timed write:
    a. Note cards
    b. Topic sentence and planning outline
    c. Working Bibliography page
    d. Brainstorming

Day 5

A. Writing Exercise:
Today's exercise will be a 30-minute timed write.

1. Using your notes and planning outline, write a paragraph defending your position on your chosen topic. Be certain to include parenthetical references for the outside material you use.

2. Develop a "Works Cited" page for your sources. It should be organized according to MLA guidelines. You may refer back to the Week 10 Lesson and to the documentation formats in Appendix D on page 202.

3. When the time is up, submit the following to your instructor:
    a. Written paragraph
    b. "Works Cited" page
    c. Working Bibliography page
    d. Planning outline
    e. Note cards

WEEK 31
Defending a Position (continued)

Daily Assignments

—————— **Day 1** ——————

A. Writing Exercise:
1. Based on the guidelines given in Week 12 Lesson, critique the following paragraph, marking scores, comments, and corrections on a grading form copied from Appendix E.

   Assignment: student choice of topic
   Type of paragraph: defending a position
   Purpose: persuade
   Audience: peers

   Listening to and learning music has been shown to have a number of effects on humans. An initial area of impact lies in the physical arena. Listening to different types of music produces varying responses in respiration, heart rates, brainwaves, and even levels of hormones which regulate the sense of well-being. "Tomatis found that the types of music most likely to promote EEG, or brainwave, patterns correlated with relaxation of muscle tension and calm attentiveness were...Baroque and classic compositions." (Wicke) Based on these physiological impacts, one can see why people use music for energizing, relaxation, intellectual stimulation and more. For instance, individuals doing aerobic exercise or other highly physical activity have used upbeat music for decades. Even stores have found that shopping patterns seem to differ based on the background music that is played. Apparently, music also produces intellectual changes in people. "Bulgarian psychologist George Lozanov found that playing Baroque instrumental music in the background while teaching foreign language vocabulary greatly increased student's speed of learning and degree of memory retention." (Wicke) Much has been promoted in the media about a study known as the Mozart effect. This initial experiment seemed to show that listening to musical pieces by Mozart temporarily improved participants' abilities to recognize shapes and put puzzles together. (Jones) Listening to music also has an emotional impact on the listener. Evidence is shown by the rising use over the past several decades of musical therapies for all sorts of maladies. Certain types of music cause increased endorphin levels which positively affects one's sense of well-being and assists in stress management. Music is also found to have a spiritual impact. First, the actual musical score evokes a mood or aura. This is accomplished with basic musical attributes such as rhythm, tempo, melody, harmony. One can attest to this just by listening to different of types of music in which these factors are varied. Vocal music may also produce a spiritual impact. Some individuals find that listening to music which contains a positive hopeful message encourages them and removes their focus from surrounding circumstances. This is evidenced by listeners' desire to listen to songs about love, heaven, friendship, beauty, and more. By contrast, listening to music which contains negative messages seems to make some individuals depressed and agitated. "This type of music imprints an extremely violent image into people's minds..." (Olson) Since music produces such significant effects in these four areas, one should be informed as to the impact of different types of music and make careful choices.

Works Cited

Jones, Rochelle. "Mozart's nice but doesn't increase IQs." Internet. Available: <http://www.cnn.com/HEALTH/9908/25.mozart.iq/>. September, 15, 2002.

Olson, Kristian David. "The Effects of Music on the Mind." Internet. Available: <http://www.bobjanuary.com/musicmnd.htm>. September 15, 2002.

Wicke, Roger W. Ph.D. "Effects of music and sound on human health." Herbalist Review, Issue 2002 #1. Internet. Available: <www.rmhiherbal.org/review/2002-1.html>. September 15, 2002.

2. Discuss that evaluation with your instructor.

Day 2

A. Writing Exercise:

Based on your instructor's feedback, you will begin an edit week, reworking the position paragraph which you wrote in Week 29. Today, edit all form, structure, and logic problems in the paragraph. This includes points off topic, unsupported contentions, and all other points in the top section of grading form. If necessary, make a new planning outline and re-write portions which are not correct. Additionally, do more research as needed in order to support your contention more adequately.

Day 3

A. Writing Exercise:

Today, continue editing your position paragraph by correcting stylistic and impression problems. This includes sentence variety, emphasis, transitions, and all other parts in the "Impression" portion of the grading form.

Day 4

A. Writing Exercise:

Today, correct any mechanical errors in your paragraph. This includes grammar, spelling, punctuation, and informalities. Also, prepare all items needed with your re-submission, including anything not submitted the first time.

Day 5

A. Writing Exercise:
1. Again, read your work aloud and be certain that you have improved in every area which the instructor has deemed necessary. Rewrite a final draft of your paragraph.

2. Submit:

   a. Your rewritten paragraph.
   b. Any other rewritten items – ie. brainstorming, outline, etc.
   c. The evaluation form filled out by your instructor.
   d. The paragraph on which your teacher wrote corrections.
   e. Any items which you did not submit with your first paragraph.

B. Test:
Complete Week 31 Quiz over Lessons 26 and 29.

WEEK 32

Lesson: *Character Analysis*

32.1 Introduction

Standard literary components include plot, theme, setting, style, and characterization. Characterization will be the student's study over the next few weeks. A **character analysis** is a position paragraph about a character, real or fictional. The student may analyze aspects of the character, analyze the role the character plays in the story, or even analyze the author's purposes for creating the character. Whatever the contention, it must be supported by information from the book or story.

A character analysis defends a position about a character.

32.2 Choosing a character

When selecting a character to discuss, one would do best to choose a character that is complex enough to make a paragraph interesting. If the paragraph writer finds himself struggling to find enough to fill a paragraph, the character is probably too flat. "Flat" characters are simple, often possessing only one major trait. For example, a character who only tells a joke at each appearance would be a flat character. "Round" characters, in contrast, are more complex, showing a wide variety of emotions and motives, like a real person. Often they are central figures in the story, and the student will generally find it easier to write about them.

A "flat" character often possesses only one major trait.

32.3 Topic Sentence

The topic sentence must state a clear contention about the character. A single contention about the character such as, "An arrogant attitude marked William Smith's life," may be enough to fill a paragraph. However, not much analysis is involved since two or three examples will quickly prove the point. Most teachers will look for a more complex analysis, in which case the topic sentence might read:

A "round" character shows a wide variety of emotions and motives, like a real person.

> Dunn creates William Smith to be a contentious, arrogant character who cares for no one but himself.

Another approach to the topic would be to consider the role that the character plays in the story. For instance:

> Doyle uses the character of Dr. Watson to question Sherlock Holmes, thereby giving the reader insight into the solution of each mystery.

A character might also symbolize something in the story. Therefore, one might craft a topic sentence such as this:

> Jennie Smith symbolizes all that is great about Hero Gulch.

When determining a possible contention, asking some standard questions can be helpful.

- Why does the character act the way he or she does?
- Who or what affected the character?
- Who or what did the character affect?
- What lessons did the author make the character learn?
- Did the character respond to such lessons?
- Was there growth or a change in the character?
- How did other characters see this character?
- How did the author use the character?
- To what extent is the character developed?
- What can we learn from the character?

32.4 Supporting information

Supporting information in a character analysis backs the contention by offering information about the character. The first point to remember when developing this type of paragraph is that supporting information should be presented in whatever order the contentions are presented in the topic sentence. For instance, using the topic sentence, "Dunn created William Smith to be a contentious, arrogant character who cared for no one but himself," the writer must first prove the character to be "contentious," then prove "arrogance," and lastly prove that he "cared for no one else but himself."

In addition to logical flow, most proof must come from the **primary source**, the book itself. Outside sources, **secondary sources**, can be used, but only to enhance an already strong case. If sufficient information is not found within the story, the chosen character is not a good one to analyze. The following list suggests many ways one may find supporting information about a character. From the information gathered by these various avenues, only the strongest points should be offered as proof of the contention.

A primary source is the original work or first hand observation, thus it contains the strongest evidence.

A secondary source is an observation or report about the original work or experience.

- Words spoken by the character
- Appearance or attire of the character
- Thoughts, actions, motivations of the character
- Moral character, strengths, virtues, vices
- Change in the character during the story
- Other character's comments about the individual
- Reactions of this individual to other characters
- Reactions of other characters to this individual
- Comparison of characters who have similarities to one another
- Contrast of characters set in opposition to one another
- Comments a narrator makes about the individual
- Setting in which the author places him/her
- Comments the author makes about the character
- Purpose of the character in the story

Thirdly, while quotations must be drawn from the primary source, a character analysis should not be a paragraph of quotations. The student's own ideas and opinions about the character must fill the body of the paragraph, with quotes added for support. A well-written character analysis should make the reader feel that the author of the analysis has given special insight into the character.

Finally, when discussing a fictional character, one should do so in the present tense, as if the character exists at this moment. For example the writer would say, "Sydney Carton is a shallow character whose only positive deed is his sacrifice for Lucy Manette." Following this topic sentence, the paragraph would continue to speak of the characters in present tense. Real people who are no longer living may be discussed in past tense.

32.5 Concluding sentence

Since a character analysis often looks at various aspects of a character, a summation serves as a good concluding sentence. A stronger option, because this is a position paragraph, is to appeal for the reader to consider the points or to explore the character or book for himself.

32A - Character Analysis Paragraph - Sample 1

Daniel Defoe uses Robinson Crusoe's rejection of authority and subsequent reaction to consequences to establish the character's rebellious, self-centered nature. First, Defoe lets the reader know that Crusoe's two brothers are dead or lost, so, with only one son left, the parents are against their youngest child's leaving to be a sailor. Selfishly unhappy with his seemingly boring life, the young man ignores his broken-hearted parents (Defoe 31). He leaves home, and they never see or hear from him again. Crusoe's disobedient heart is further shown by his rejection of consequences. A major storm threatens his ship followed by a second storm which sinks his ship, yet Crusoe refuses to surrender his will and excuses his own actions. When he reaches safety, the willful young man is even warned by the father of a friend that his actions will result in "disasters and disappointments" (Defoe 11). Following these two storms, Crusoe boards yet another ship which is captured by pirates. He is taken prisoner in Sallee and made a slave; rather than repent, the strong-willed Crusoe relies on his cleverness for escape. Thus did Defoe craft pleas, admonitions, consequences, and prophetic warnings, all of which went unheeded by his famous, selfish character who, ultimately, is only changed by decades of isolation.

Works Cited

Defoe, Daniel. *Robinson Crusoe.* New York: Everyman's Library, 1992.

32B - Character Analysis Paragraphs - Samples 2 & 3

L. M. Montgomery uses the character of Anne Shirley to transform two static characters into dynamic personalities. Matthew Cuthbert, the first person Anne meets, changes profoundly as a result of her coming. Matthew Cuthbert is a quiet, introverted man who has worked the family farm for decades. Due to his advancing age, Matthew rationally decides to adopt a boy to help him around the farm. Since Matthew finds communicating with females difficult, one can imagine his discomfort when he arrives to find a girl rather than a boy. Her arrival forces him to deal with Anne's needs and changes him from a retiring person into a father figure. For instance, when Marilla grounds Anne from a Sunday School picnic, he encourages Anne to take proper actions to right her relationship with his sister. He also becomes the orphan's confidant, and she comes to care for him deeply. Anne's arrival also changes his lifelong relationship with his sister. Generally content to let Marilla make the decisions, he confronts her harsh punishment of Anne and encourages her to be kind to the girl. He purchases Anne chocolates for a treat and even buys a pretty dress for Anne when he sees that Marilla's choice of austere clothing does not fit with the prevailing style. When Anne wants to attend a late night concert at her friend's house and Marilla does not approve, Matthew intervenes. Anne is allowed to go. Matthew becomes Anne's greatest encourager. Even giving up his dream of adopting a boy and realizing that he will have to continue doing the heavy labor is a point of growth for Matthew.

Marilla, Matthew's unmarried sister, also grows a great deal as a result of Anne's coming to Avonlea. She is a woman who has led a hard life and along with her brother has settled into a routine of grinding duties. Yearning for beauty is far from her mind, so when Anne begins to change the stark room at their house into a warm, welcoming place, Marilla is amazed and over time begins to see life through different eyes. A woman of strict standards, she metes out harsh punishment to Anne. Marilla accuses Anne of stealing a brooch and punishes Anne by grounding her. When Marilla finds the missing brooch and realizes that she has wrongly accused Anne, she is faced with her own prejudices against the orphan, and again her attitude changes for the better. Marilla is accustomed to holding in her emotions, while Anne freely dispenses impulsive hugs and love. On occasions when Marilla grants Anne freedoms or acts kindly toward Anne, the orphan girl spontaneously throws her arms around the old woman. In another impulsive moment, Anne secretly applies hair dye that she has smuggled into the house; it accidentally turns her hair green. Marilla cannot help chuckling at the child's silliness. Gradually her staunch reserve softens to Anne's expressiveness and childish simplicity. Even Marilla's social interaction changes because of Anne. For example, at Anne's request, Matthew and Marilla attend a Christmas concert for the first time in twenty years. Montgomery crafted two characters who would have remained unchanged except for the character of Anne Shirley.

Works Consulted

Montgomery, Lucy Maude. *Anne of Green Gables*. New York: Bantam Books, 1981.

32C - Example Character Analysis Topic Sentences

Topic Idea	Position to Defend
Interactions with others	Each time Brenden interacts with his peers, he better learns how to work with them.
	Steven's character, Loretta, works very hard at honoring her parents.
Consequences of a character's actions	Respect from his superiors results from Art's conscientious work ethic.
A character's growth or progression	The king's efforts do not produce the desired results until he follows the advice of his counselors.
Extent of a character's change	Bob's tendencies to be financially irresponsible diminish, but he still has trouble following a strict budget.
	Outwardly, Joe acts as if he has changed, but inwardly his negative thought patterns continue.
	Joan successfully overcomes the difficulties she faces.
Cause of a character's change	Losing his job makes Bob consider how he might become a better employee.
A character's flaws	Angel tries to conduct herself more in keeping with her name, but she fails to act properly.
The impact of other people upon this character	Praise and encouragement from her father help Naomi believe that she can achieve her goals.
Motives of a character	Sinister motives seem to be the only driving force behind each of Chuck's friendships.
Extent of a character's development	Jones creates, in Hannah, a well-developed character with which the audience can identify.
	Andrew's character, Falwood, is not fully-developed, so the reader cannot connect with him.

WEEK 32
Character Analysis

Daily Assignments

―――――― **Day 1** ――――――

A. Reading Assignment:
Study the Week 32 lesson on writing a character analysis paragraph thoroughly.

B. Lesson Exercise:
Answer the following questions in complete sentences:
1. How does one chose a strong character for discussion?
2. If the writer offers a listing of contentions in his topic sentence, how must the paragraph be developed?
3. What is the primary source of proof in a character analysis?
4. In what verb tense should a fictional character be discussed?
5. What might make a strong ending for a character analysis paragraph?

C. Writing Exercise:
1. *Brainstorm a topic for a character analysis. Remember that you will need to take a strong position about this character. Choose a character from a book you have already read, thus you can spend your time this week writing rather than reading. Write your brainstorming list neatly, in a manner that is suitable for submission with your final draft.*

   Assignment: character analysis of fictional character
   Purpose: to persuade
   Audience: someone who may know a little about your book
   Topic suggestions: any sufficiently developed fictional character

2. *Write a preliminary topic sentence that states your contention about the character and begin your research for supporting evidence. To prove your contention, you will use information, examples, or other material from the book(s). You must include two quotes from the primary source and may add one from a secondary source, if you desire. Again, your research will need to be properly documented.*

3. *Begin forming a planning outline for this character analysis paragraph. On your outline, identify the logical proofs you are using.*

―――――― **Day 2** ――――――

A. Writing Exercise:
1. *Formulate a final topic sentence and complete your planning outline. Create a copy of your outline to be submitted to your instructor with your final draft.*

2. Draft the entire character analysis paragraph. Up to two literary devices, chosen by the student from those introduced in this course, may be added to this assignment for extra credit. They may be worked in any time between now and Day 4.

3. Create a copy of your paragraph draft today, so that you can mark corrections on it tomorrow. This corrected copy will be submitted with your final draft on Day 5.

Day 3

A. Writing Exercise:
1. Now begin to edit your paragraph draft from yesterday, marking corrections and changes on your rough draft.

2. If you find it necessary, do more research and revise your planning outline. Create a new copy of the outline for submission.

3. Add three different style points on this day.

4. Prepare a revised copy of your paragraph.

Day 4

A. Writing Exercise:
1. Go over your paragraph and correct all spelling, punctuation, and grammatical errors.

2. Today is the final day to add one or two literary devices for extra credit. In order to receive full credit, you must work them in to your paragraph and clearly mark them. No separate samples will be accepted this week.

3. Make other improvements according to standard guidelines.

4. Prepare a revised draft of your paragraph.

Day 5

A. Writing Exercise:
1. The final day to polish your paragraph has come. Read the paragraph aloud slowly and listen for problem areas. Now, have someone else read it to you so that you can listen and be certain that the product is well-written.

2. Using the Paragraph Checklist, review your paragraph. Check off each guideline in the upper section when you have verified that you have followed it. In the lower section, mark the style points you have used. On your final draft, identify these style points by writing the corresponding number from the checklist directly above each one, and label the literary device.

3. *Make certain that the text includes appropriate parenthetical references in-text, and that the "Works Cited" page and "Works Consulted" page, if required, are complete.*
4. *Make certain that the assignment is properly formatted.*
5. *Submit your work to the instructor:*
    a. *Final paragraph draft*
    b. *"Works Cited" page*
    c. *"Works Consulted" page, as applicable*
    d. *Paragraph checklist*
    e. *All drafts*
    f. *Topic sentence & planning outline*
    g. *Brainstorming*

WEEK 33
Character Analysis (Continued)

Daily Assignments

——— Day 1 ———

A. Writing Exercise:

This week you will prepare for a timed writing of a character analysis paragraph on Day 5. Research and gather bibliographic information in preparation for writing your paragraph.. To prove your contention, you will use examples or other material from the original source, and you may use one other outside source, if you desire.

Today, brainstorm possible characters for analysis. Using the primary source in which the character is portrayed, take general notes as needed on the character. Record any quotations, summaries, or paraphrases you might use to support your topic on note cards. Be certain to gather necessary bibliographic information. The paragraph must contain at least one quotation from the primary source, but no more than three.

Topic: student choice
Purpose: persuade
Audience: a person interested in reading the work
Suggested topic: any fictional character

——— Day 2 ———

A. Writing Exercise:

1. *Continue to research your topic and obtain at least six quotes, summaries, or paraphrases for possible use.*

2. *Continue developing a list of the bibliographic information which corresponds to your notes. On the day you write your paragraph, you will draw from this list for your "Works Cited" page. Naturally, only the sources you use in your paragraph will be cited on the "Works Cited" page. General or common knowledge gleaned from your sources need not be specifically cited.*

——— Day 3 ———

A. Writing Exercise:

1. *Complete your research.*

2. *Brainstorm supporting points from your research and your own knowledge about the topic.*

3. *Formulate a final topic sentence and begin a planning outline for your paragraph. On your outline, identify the logical proofs you are using.*

———— Day 4 ————

A. Writing Exercise:

1. Of the quotes you compiled, you may use two to three in this paragraph. The remainder of the paragraph must be your own work. Your use of the outside material should work to support the contention stated by your topic sentence. Today, determine which quotes you will use and complete your planning outline. On your outline, identify the logical proofs you are using. <u>You may not pre-write your paragraph.</u>

2. Create a Working Bibliography for all the sources you studied. <u>Do not create the "Works Cited" page.</u>

3. Gather all materials which you will need for tomorrow's timed write:

    a. Notes
    b. Topic sentence and planning outline
    c. Working Bibliography page
    d. Brainstorming

———— Day 5 ————

A. Writing Exercise:
Today's exercise will be a 30-minute timed write.

1. Using your notes and planning outline, write a paragraph defending your position on your chosen topic. Be certain to include parenthetical references for the outside material you use.

    Length: 12 or more sentences
    Purpose: to persuade
    Audience: a person interested in reading the work

2. Develop a "Works Cited" page for your sources. It should be organized according to MLA guidelines. You may refer back to the Week 10 Lesson and to the documentation formats in Appendix D on page 202.

3. When the time is up, submit the following to your instructor:

    a. Written paragraph
    b. "Works Cited" page
    c. Working Bibliography page
    d. Planning outline
    e. Brainstorming
    f. Notes, quotations and other source material

WEEK 34
Character Analysis (continued)

Daily Assignments

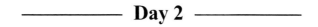

Day 1

A. Writing Exercise:
1. Based on the guidelines given in Week 12 Lesson, critique the following paragraph, marking scores, comments, and corrections on a grading form copied from Appendix E.

   Assignment: analyze a fictional character
   Type of paragraph: character analysis
   Purpose: persuade
   Audience: a person interested in reading the work

   Anne Shirley is a character in a book entitled Anne of Green Gables. Anne possesses an unbelievable imagination. She is always dreaming of herself as being royalty. She is an orphan, so she imagines having a family. Anne is also stubborn and willful. She struggles to submit to those in authority over her. Whether it is her teacher or her guardians. She struggles with accepting her appearance. Her red hair and freckles bother her and she wishes for a more glamorous appearance. Anne's flair for the dramatic gets her into positive and negative situations. Sometimes her dramatics lead to others thinking she is in crisis. Anne also has opportunity to deliver dramatic poetry. Finally, Anne is a loyal and loving person. She is loyal and appreciative of Marilla and Matthew who have taken her into their home. Anne is a fun girl whom many readers have come to love.

2. Discuss that evaluation with your instructor.

Day 2

A. Writing Exercise:
Based on your instructor's feedback, begin to edit the position paragraph which you wrote in Week 32. Today, edit all form, structure, and logic problems in the paragraph. This includes points off topic, unsupported contentions, and all other points in the top section of grading form. If necessary, make a new planning outline and re-write portions which are not correct. Additionally, do more research as needed in order to support your contention more adequately.

Day 3

A. Writing Exercise:
Today, continue editing your position paragraph by correcting stylistic and impression problems. This includes sentence variety, emphasis, transitions, and all other parts in the "Impression" portion of the grading form.

Day 4

A. Writing Exercise:
Today, correct any mechanical errors in your paragraph. This includes grammar, spelling, punctuation, and informalities. Also, prepare all items needed with your re-submission, including anything not submitted the first time.

Day 5

A. Writing Exercise:
1. *Again, read your work aloud and be certain that you have improved in every area which the instructor has deemed necessary. Rewrite a final draft of your paragraph.*
2. *Submit:*
    a. *Your rewritten paragraph.*
    b. *Any other rewritten items – ie. brainstorming, outline, etc.*
    c. *The evaluation form filled out by your instructor.*
    d. *The paragraph on which your teacher wrote corrections.*
    e. *Any items which you did not submit with your first paragraph.*

WEEK 35

Lesson: *Seeing the Big Picture*

35.1 Introduction

In order to understand how the teachings of this course fit into the larger picture, it will be beneficial to look at how language develops. Spoken language develops in a progressive fashion. Sounds become words; words become sentences. Each component works as a building block for the next level of language use. Likewise, students learning to read must master the first level: phonics. Next, they read words, followed by sentences, then stories. In the same way, the writer must progress from words to sentences and then to paragraphs, the focus of this course. The next step is to see that paragraphs are the building blocks for larger works such as essays. In order to understand how standard paragraphs fit together to form an essay, the components of a five-paragraph essay are listed in Illustration 35A.

35A Five Paragraph Essay Outline

1. *Introduction paragraph*
   a. *Attention getter*
   b. *Narrowing statements*
   c. *Thesis statement - with path statement*

2. *Body paragraph #1*
   a. *Topic sentence*
   b. *Supporting material*
   c. *Concluding sentence*

3. *Body paragraph #2*
   a. *Topic sentence*
   b. *Supporting material*
   c. *Concluding sentence*

4. *Body paragraph #3*
   a. *Topic sentence*
   b. *Supporting material*
   c. *Concluding sentence*

5. *Conclusion paragraph*
   a. *Thesis restatement*
   b. *Restate body paragraph #1*
   c. *Restate body paragraph #2*
   d. *Restate body paragraph #3*
   e. *Conclusion or appeal*

If one looks carefully at the components listed above, it will be clear that the paragraph forms learned in this course make up those that form the *body* of an essay. They began with a topic sentence, followed by supporting information, and ended with a concluding sentence. In an essay, the *introduction* and *conclusion* paragraphs follow a different pattern.

35.2 Essay Introduction

When creating a standard essay, an introductory paragraph will begin the composition. This paragraph is different than those studied previously in this course. First, it begins with a general opening statement rather than a topic sentence. Frequently, this opener is an "attention getter," a statement designed to capture the attention of or even startle the reader. Next, comes a series of narrowing statements which progressively move the reader in a few sentences to the specific topic under consideration. Finally, the last sentence of the introductory paragraph, known as the **thesis statement**, establishes the exact goal for the essay. Often, the thesis statement will include a list of the general topics to be covered in each of the body paragraphs. This list is given different names in various curricula: plan of attack, path statement, or supporting points. Like the topic sentence in a paragraph, the thesis statement sets the purpose and the tone for the paper.

> *A thesis statement is a single sentence which establishes the exact goal of the essay.*

35.3 Essay Body

An academic essay usually contains at least three body paragraphs which present the logical arguments in support of the thesis. Longer essays and research papers, while still including an introduction and conclusion, contain many more paragraphs. An important difference with body paragraphs in essays is that the topic sentences should begin with transitions. These lead the reader smoothly to each new idea discussed. The paragraphs themselves should progress from weakest to strongest argument, just as should the supporting information within each paragraph. Therefore, regardless of the length, strong content combined with great transitions make for an outstanding essay.

35.4 Essay Conclusion

The conclusion of an essay follows a specific standard form. First, the thesis offers the same contention restated in a new way. Following that, each of the body paragraphs is summarized, using a single sentence for each body paragraph. The writer must not introduce new topics not covered in the body of the essay. To conclude the essay, one may offer a generality about the topic, an appeal, a conclusion, a question, or a quotation. This conclusion sums up the case one last time for the reader.

Addendum - Week 35

Sample Essay - to Demonstrate Form

Introduction

    What exciting recreational activity beckons you whenever you have free time on your hands? Different individuals handle this lull in the action of their lives in a variety of ways. For example, some squander the time as "couch potatoes," while others choose to become involved in pastimes that are either physically or mentally stimulating. Currently one particular activity, snowboarding, has become one of the world's favorite recreations. When an individual acquires the necessary equipment, discovers a suitable location, and masters basic skills, snowboarding becomes an enjoyable pastime.

Body Paragraph #1

    In order for snowboarding to become an exciting recreational activity, an individual pursuing this pastime must, first, procure the essential equipment. The most important piece of equipment is the snowboard, which is similar in design and construction to the snow ski, with the exception that the width differs to allow for a sideways stance on the board. Manufacturers make the boards in a variety of lengths and widths, designing each one specifically for different styles of riding, body weight, and height. Once these variable factors are determined, individuals are able to choose a snowboard that most clearly meets their needs for freestyle, free riding, free carving, racing, or slalom snowboarding. In addition to the board, one must select the right bindings which "clip" snowboard boots onto the board. From freestyle to racing, and from racing to step-ins, each binding and boot is designed for a specific purpose. The flexibility afforded by using freestyle boots allows halfpipe riders to perform more precise stunts; the hard plastic shell of racing boots provides greater support for extreme moves in back country and alpine conditions, and the technology offered by step-in boots permits greater ease of strapping on the snowboard. After this essential equipment has been acquired, an individual is ready to "surf" the fresh, powdery snow.

Body Paragraph #2

    Once proper equipment is obtained, an individual must find a location that is enjoyable and suitable for his skill level in order for snowboarding to become a pleasant free-time activity. Ski resorts across America, from the east coast to the west coast, often provide convenient, safe, and exciting places to put snowboarding skills to the test. The advantages of a resort include the convenience offered by chairlifts, groomed trails, professional instruction, and the proximity of food and lodging. For beginners, as well as seasoned professionals, these amenities contribute significantly to creating an enjoyable atmosphere. In addition, the aspect of safety is of great importance at resorts so that snowboarders can leave their fears of injury at home and have a safe place to gain experience. To ensure safety on the ski slopes, the resort's ski patrol informs boarders of weather conditions and keeps an eye on potential avalanche situations, while trail markings indicate routes with steep terrain and dangerous obstacles. Finally, regardless of the individual's skill level, the various ski runs offered at resorts allow every snowboarder an equally exciting downhill experience. Jumps and obstacles are available for advanced boarders, and gentle sloping hills are available for beginners to negotiate. Because ski resorts provide snowboarders with special amenities, safeguards against a myriad of dangers, and a variety of ski runs, snowboarders of all skill levels can have a great time.

Body Paragraph #3

Finally, mastery of basic skills and techniques, which allow an individual to perform fundamental maneuvers, is essential if a snowboarder is to truly enjoy the sport. Once a person determines which is more comfortable, a regular or "goofy" stance, the first important technique one must learn is the heel-side to toe-side move. When performing a heel-side move, the edge of the board under one's heels is used to control speed and manage turns, while in the toe-side move, it is the edge under one's toes by which speed and turns in the opposite direction are controlled. Changing from heel-side to toe-side and back again is accomplished by leaning in the desired direction while maintaining slightly bent legs. After this technique is mastered and the individual is able to make controlled turns and come to safe stops, the doors are opened to attempt simple tricks. The ollie, a simple jump, which may be used on flat ground or to gain more height off a ramp, is the easiest jumping maneuver to learn. To perform this maneuver, an individual leans back on the tail of the board, once a comfortable speed is achieved, then pushes off the ground; legs must be bent for smooth landings. This maneuver is critical to learn for one to feel confident and in control on the slopes. Also, more advanced tricks such as ollie grabs, 360's, and flips involve this jump in one way or another. Once mastered, these fundamental skills allow individuals to fully appreciate this popular winter sport.

Conclusion

Many individuals, after completing three preliminary steps, consider snowboarding an enjoyable pastime. Having first acquired a snowboard, boots, and bindings appropriate for a particular style of snowboarding, they are equipped to experience the joys of the sport. A thoughtfully selected ski resort offering desired amenities, important safeguards, and appropriate ski runs enhances the pleasure. Lastly, the mastery of basic skills not only makes snowboarding more enjoyable, but it also establishes a foundation for learning more advanced maneuvers in the future. When determining how to spend your free time, why not grab your hat and gloves and head for the mountains to enjoy the thrilling sport of snowboarding?

WEEK 35
Seeing the Big Picture

Daily Assignments

--- **Day 1** ---

A. Reading Assignment:
Read the Week 35 Lesson carefully, being certain to understand how standard paragraphs fit into a larger essay.

B. Lesson Exercise:
Answer the following questions in complete sentences:

1. Essays begin with what kind of paragraph?
2. What is a thesis statement?
3. What is the purpose of body paragraphs?
4. How many <u>body</u> paragraphs are in a typical academic essay?
5. What gets restated in the concluding paragraph?
6. What is the purpose of the concluding paragraph?

C. Writing Exercise:

1. *Read the partially developed essay below. Note that <u>only</u> two of the three needed body paragraphs are written. Considering the thesis carefully, decide on a third point to develop into a body paragraph for this essay.*

2. *Brainstorm the content of a third paragraph for this essay. Supporting evidence must come from different literary works than those used in the first two paragraphs. Print your brainstorming list for this paragraph neatly for submission on Day 5. If necessary, research the topic for sufficient information. Organize and document your research for submission with your final work.*

   Topic: student choice
   Purpose: to persuade
   Audience: instructor

3. *Write a topic sentence and create a planning outline for this week's paragraph. Print a copy of your outline to be submitted to your instructor with your final draft.*

Sample Essay

Introduction
   What areas of interest consume all of your free time? Some might say the movies, others enjoy sports, and interestingly, some might talk of their love of books. When reading books, one will discover certain characteristics which he personally desires in a book. In general, a carefully chosen setting, engaging characters, and _____(student choice)_____ add to the pleasing nature of a book.

Body Paragraph #1

The story line of a satisfying book usually takes place in a well-chosen setting. Setting involves both physical surroundings and the time in which the action takes place. The physical world in which the characters move must be imaginable to the reader. For instance, the primary action in Dickens' A Tale of Two Cities takes place in France, in a suburb of Paris called Saint Antoine. Dickens' description of the physical setting also gives allusion to the historical setting.

> And now that the cloud settled on Saint Antoine, which a momentary gleam had driven from his sacred countenance, the darkness of it was heavy - cold, dirt, sickness, ignorance, and want,... - nobles of great power all of them; but, most especially the last...Samples of a people that had undergone a terrible grinding and re-grinding in the mill, ...the mill that grinds young people old...Its abiding place was in all things fitted to it. A narrow winding street, full of offence and stench...Across the streets, at wide intervals, one clumsy lamp was slung by a rope and pulley;...a feeble grove of dim wicks swung in a sickly manner overhead, as if they were at sea. Indeed they were at sea, and the ship and crew were in peril of tempest (Dickens 26-27).

The darkness of this time in France is reflected in Dickens' description of the depressed conditions of Saint Antoine. The French aristocrats' disdainful treatment of peasants is causing anger which, like a pressure cooker building steam, is rising to a crisis point. The "tempest" is ignited when the citizens storm the Bastille. Dickens' portrayal of a sad story during the French Revolution is enhanced by placing it in depressing surroundings during dark days. Like Dickens, every author determines which setting might best enhance his story. From current day, to centuries in the future, to a historical past, an appropriate setting will "frame" the story.

Body Paragraph #2

Along with an appropriate setting, excellent books usually include appealing characters. Often a strong character exhibits traits which endear the reader to him. Many readers will identify with an innocent child who faces adversity or a person of integrity who stands for the right. Another type of character with which the reader can relate might demonstrate a flaw that must be overcome. One such character, Eustace, is presented in The Voyage of the "Dawn Treader" by C.S. Lewis. This self-centered, cantankerous lad is visited by his cousins, Lucy and Edmund, who have already been to Narnia and back. He makes it clear to these relatives that he does not like them and has no desire to be with them. Eustace's bad attitude only continues when the children find themselves drawn into a picture and dumped into the Narnian Sea. Naturally, Eustace shows no gratitude when Prince Caspian and his sailors pluck him from the water and take him aboard their ship, the <u>Dawn Treader</u>. On board, Eustace plots, sulks, and acts disgustingly. Finally, there comes a point in the story when Eustace is transformed into a huge dragon. The young lad sees himself for the monster he really is, and when given an opportunity to become a boy again, he changes for the better. This dramatic transformation endears Eustace to the reader. What a delight creative characters can be (Lewis).

Body Paragraph #3

To be written by student according to instructions.

Conclusion

Three features combine to enhance the appeal of a book. First, a story set within a fitting time and place serves to engage the reader. Additionally, characters with interesting qualities and experiences further draw the reader into the book. _____(student choice)_____. The next time you are looking for a way to enjoy some free time, choose a book which has these important attributes.

Works Cited

Dickens, Charles. A Tale of Two Cities. New York: Bantam Books, 1981.

Lewis, C.S. Voyage of the "Dawn Treader." New York: Macmillan Publishing, 1952.

Day 2

A. **Style Drill:**
Identify any style points used in Body Paragraphs #1 and #2 of the above sample essay.

B. **Writing Exercise:**
Draft the entire third body paragraph which you planned on Day 1. Work at least three style points into this paragraph. Also, one literary device learned this year must be employed in this paragraph and may be worked in any time between now and Day 4. If you find it necessary, revise your planning outline and write a new copy for submission. Otherwise, complete this first draft of your paragraph so that you can mark corrections on it tomorrow. This corrected copy will be submitted with your final draft on Day 5.

Day 3

A. **Writing Exercise:**
 1. *Now, begin to edit your paragraph draft from yesterday, marking corrections and changes on your rough draft. Stick with the following guidelines:*
    a. *For this body paragraph, use supporting evidence from different works than referenced in the first two body paragraphs.*
    b. *Continue creating sentences which vary in structure. Be certain that you have used three style points by this day.*
    c. *Think about where you can insert a literary device,*
 2. *Create another copy of this revision for submission on Day 5.*

Day 4

A. **Writing Exercise:**
 1. *Go over your paragraph and correct all spelling, punctuation, and grammatical errors.*
 2. *A literary device must be added to the paragraph by this day. Not optional.*
 3. *Make other improvements in words and phrases that may come to mind.*
 4. *Prepare a revised draft of your paragraph.*

Day 5

A. Writing Exercise:

1. *The final day to polish your paragraph has come. Read the paragraph aloud slowly and listen for problem areas. Now, have someone else read it to you so that you can listen and be certain that the product is well-written.*

2. *Using the paragraph checklist, review your paragraph to be certain that you have followed the guidelines in the upper section. In the lower section, check off the style points you have used, and mark them on your paper with appropriate numbers directly above each style point on the checklist.*

3. *Make certain that the text includes appropriate parenthetical citations in text, and that the "Works Cited" page is complete.*

4. *Make certain that the assignment is double-spaced, has one inch margins, has page numbering if needed, and that it includes the proper heading required by your instructor.*

5. *Submit your work to the instructor in this order:*
   a. *Final draft paragraph*
   b. *"Works Cited" page*
   c. *Paragraph checklist*
   d. *All drafts*
   e. *Topic sentence & planning outline*
   f. *Brainstorming*

WEEK 36

Daily Assignments

──────── **Final Week** ────────

A. Test:
Complete the comprehensive Week 36 Final Exam. Study of previous tests is recommended.

Appendixes

APPENDIX A

State of Being Verbs							
am	are	was	were	be	been	being	is

Helping (Auxiliary) Verbs							
have	had	does	can	shall	will	may	must
has	do	did	could	should	would	might	

Common Conjunctive Adverbs					
again	consequently	hence	likewise	nonetheless	then
also	conversely	however	meanwhile	otherwise	thereafter
accordingly	finally	in addition	moreover	similarly	therefore
besides	further	indeed	nevertheless	still	thereupon
certainly	furthermore	instead	next	subsequently	thus

Common Subordinating Conjunctions					
after	as though	in order that	so that	until	whether
although	because	lest	than	when	while
as	before	once	that	whenever	why
as if	even if	provided that	though	where	
as much as	even though	rather than	til	whereas	
as long as	if	since	unless	wherever	

APPENDIX B

Prepositions List

about	before	during	on	toward
above	behind	except	onto	under
across	below	for	out	underneath
after	beneath	from	outside	until
against	beside	in	over	up
along	between	inside	past	upon
amid	beyond	into	regarding	with
among	but	like	since	within
around	by	near	through	without
at	concerning	of	throughout	
atop	down	off	to	

Style Point Reference List

Variety of Opening Words:
   S1 - Opening Adverb ("ly")
   Thankfully, his child was not injured.
   S2 - Opening Participle
   Running, he tripped and fell.

Variety of Opening Phrases:
   S3 - Opening Participial Phrase
   Present: *Running for his life, he tripped and fell.*
   Past: *Finished with his dinner, the boy ran outside to play.*
   S4 - Opening Prepositional Phrase
   For the sake of the baby monkey, zoo keepers closed the exhibit.
   S5 - Opening Infinitive Phrase
   To run in the Hood to Coast race is a lifetime goal for many.

Variety of Clauses:
   S6 - Opening Adverbial Clause
   While the stunned family watched, the dog jumped onto the table.
   S7 - Adjective clause
   The dress, which her mother made, fit perfectly.

Altering Traditional Word Order:
   S8 - Reversed order of subject and verb.
   Onto the driveway rolled the car.

Formality and Grammar Reference List

- Contractions
- Colloquial Wording
- Slang
- Cliché
- First & Second Person
- Sentence Fragments
- Ending with a Preposition
- Nominalizations
- Spelling & Punctuation
- Subject - Verb Agreement
- Verb tense consistency
- Antecedent clarity
- Person and Number Consistency
- Use Active Voice

APPENDIX C

Paragraph Checklist

To be submitted with paragraphs written during Weeks 9, 11, 14, 17, 20, 23, 26, 29, 32, and 35

For grading purposes, award one-half point for each of the following items.

Structure

- ☐ I have a clearly developed outline.
- ☐ I have an accurate and concise topic sentence.
- ☐ All supporting sentences are topical to the topic sentence.
- ☐ My ideas are developed clearly and logically.
- ☐ I have placed subordinate ideas in subordinate construction.
- ☐ I have a proper concluding sentence.

Grammatical Guidelines

- ☐ I have corrected all spelling and punctuation errors.
- ☐ I have kept subjects and verbs in agreement.
- ☐ I have kept verb tenses consistent.
- ☐ Antecedents of pronouns are clear.
- ☐ Person and number are consistent.
- ☐ I have written as many sentences as possible in active voice.

General Guidelines

- ☐ I have eliminated contractions, colloquial wording, slang, and clichés.
- ☐ I have written with the appropriate level of formality.
- ☐ I have eliminated sentence fragments and nominalization.

Style

- ☐ I have used precise words: adjectives, adverbs, verbs, and nouns.
- ☐ I have varied sentence patterns:
  - simple, compound, complex, compound-complex
  - variety of opening words, phrases, clauses.
  - occasionally altered traditional word order.
- ☐ I have fully developed ideas so the reader understands and pictures my point.
- ☐ I have used transition words and phrases in order to help the reader follow my logic.
- ☐ I have used the assigned literary device.

Style Point Checklist

For grading purposes, award one point per style point used each week.

Style Points – as explained in Week 7, Paragraph Basics 2

- ☐ S1 Opening adverb.
- ☐ S2 Opening participle.
- ☐ S3 Opening participle phrase.
- ☐ S4 Opening prepositional phrase.
- ☐ S5 Opening infinitive phrase.
- ☐ S6 Opening adverbial clause.
- ☐ S7 Adjective clause.
- ☐ S8 Altering traditional word order.

APPENDIX D

Example Citations

The following additional notations are to be added to the citations on the Works Cited or Works Consulted pages according to the instructions.

- **Missing information:**

    If information cannot be found, appropriate symbols should be inserted into the documentation at the exact point where it would have been recorded.

    n.p. – *no place of publication given*
    n.p. – *no publisher given*
    n.d. – *no date of publication given*
    n. pag. – *no pagination given*

- **Editions:**

    If the edition used is other than the first edition, appropriate notation of the edition should be inserted before the city of publication in each case.

    Examples:
    2nd ed.
    Rev. ed. - *revised edition*
    Abr. ed. - *abridged edition*
    1995 ed. - *year of edition*

Type of Source	Sample In-Text Citation	Appearance on "Works Cited" Page
Book by a single author	(Doub 123)	*Format:* Author's last name, first name and middle name or initial (if any). *Book Title* (underlined or italicized). City of publication: Publisher, Date of publication. *Example:* Doub, William C. *History of the United States.* San Francisco: Doub & Company, 1927.
Book by two or three authors	(Corbett 83)	*Format:* First author's last name, first name and middle name or initial (if any), and second author's first, middle, and last name. *Book Title* (underlined or italicized). City of publication: Publisher, Date of publication. *Example:* Corbett, Edward P.J., Robert J. Connors. *Classical Rhetoric for the Modern Student.* 4th ed. New York: Oxford University Press, 1999.
Book by more than three authors	(Hicks, et al. 18)	*Format:* First author's last name, first name, et al. *Book Title* (underlined or italicized). City of publication: Publisher, Date of publication. *Example:* Hicks, Laurel, et al. *American Government and Economics in Christian Perspective.* Pensacola: A Beka, 1984.
Book by group or corporate author (most textbooks)	(Mike Roberts Color Productions 33)	*Format:* Name of group or corporation. *Book Title* (underlined or italicized). City of publication: Publisher, Date of publication. *Example*: Mike Roberts Color Productions. *American Revolution Bicentennial.* Berkeley: Mike Roberts Color Productions, 1975.

Example Citations (continued)

Type of Source	Sample In-Text Citation	Appearance on "Works Cited" Page
Two books by the same author	(Elliot, "*Path*" 98) (Elliot, "*Music*" 120)	*Example: (Books are arranged alphabetically by title.)* Elliot, Elisabeth. *The Music of His Promises*. Ann Arbor: Servant Publications, 2000. ---. *A Path Through Suffering*. Ann Arbor: Servant Publications, 1990.
Multi-volume reference book (includes dictionaries and encyclopedias)	(Brittannica 18:688) *Note: Indicates volume 18 and page 688*	*Format:* "Word reference." *Encyclopedia Title* (underlined or italicized). Editor (if any). Edition. City of publication: Publisher, Date of publication. *Example:* "Trees." *Encyclopedia Brittannica*. 15th ed. Chicago: William Benton, Publisher, 1979.
Single-volume reference book (includes dictionaries and encyclopedias)	(Webster's 199)	*Format:* "Word reference." *Encyclopedia Title* (underlined or italicized). Editor (if any). Edition. City of publication: Publisher, Date of publication. *Example:* "Humble." *Webster's High School Dictionary*. Springfield: American Book Company, Publisher, 1892. (no editor was listed)
Anthology	(Spenser 1336)	*Format:* Last name of author of work in anthology, first name and middle name or initial (if any). "Title of Work." *Book Title*. Ed (if any). First name and last name. City of publication: Publisher, Date of publication. *Example:* Spenser, Edmund. "The Faerie Queen." *World Masterpieces*. Ed. Maynard Mack. New York: W. W. Norton & Company, 1965.
Republished book	(Smith 152)	*Format:* Author's last name, first name and middle name or initial (if any). *Book Title*. Original publication date. City of current publication: Publisher, Current date of publication. *Example:* Smith, Joan A. *Field Trips Children Love*. 1983. Portland: Family Publications, 2002.
Using one volume of a multi-volume work	(Barnett 8:152) *Note: Indicates volume 8 and page 152*	*Format:* Author's last name, first name and middle name or initial (if any). *Book Title*. Ed (if any). first and last name. Volume #. City of publication: Publisher, Publication date. *Example:* Barnett, Beau. *Stories of the Great Northwest*. Ed. Jeff Barrett. Vol. 8. Vancouver: n.p. 30 Aug. 1983.
Using two or more of a mulit-volume work	(Barnett 8:152-154) *Note: Indicates volume 8 and page 152*	*Format:* Author's last name, first name and middle name or initial (if any). *Book Title*. Ed (if any). first and last name. Number of volumes in set. City of publication: Publisher,Publication date. *Example:* Barnett, Beau. *Stories of the Great Northwest*. Ed. Jeff Barrett. 9 vols. Vancouver: n.p. 30 Aug. 1983.

Example Citations (continued)

Type of Source	Sample In-Text Citation	Appearance on "Works Cited" Page
Bible	(New American Standard Bible, Jer. 29.11)	*Format:* Version of the Bible. General Editor (if any). City of Publication: Publisher, Year of publication. *Example:* New American Standard Bible. The Lockman Foundation. Nashville: Thomas Nelson, 1978.
Anonymous book	(Solving) *Note: Use first word or key word from title*	*Format:* Title of book (underlined or italicized). City of publication: Publisher, Publication date. *(Alphabetize entry on "Works Cited" page by title.)* *Example:* Solving Neighborhood Problems. Portland: Grin 'n Barrett Publications, 2002.
Anonymous article	(Developing) *Note: Use first word or key word from title*	*Format:* "Title of Article." Name of publication (underlined). Day Month and year of publication: pages on which article appears. *(Alphabetize entry on "Works Cited" page by title.)* *Example:* "Developing Strong Families." Strong Ties. 30 Aug. 1983: 27-30.
Periodical	(Mollenkamp 111)	*Format:* Author's last name, first name and middle name or initial (if any). "Title of the article in quotation marks." *Name of the journal* (underlined or italicized). Volume number, (Year): page numbers for the entire article. *Example:* Mollenkamp, Becky. "Keep Your Child's School Safe." Better Homes and Gardens. Volume 79, (2001): 111-114.
Speech or Lecture	(Wilkins)	*Format:* Speaker's last name, first name and middle name or initial. Title of speech or event. City: Date delivered. *Example:* Wilkins, J. Steven. *"Wise Words to the Young."* Lecture 3. Vancouver: 23 Aug. 2000.
Film or video	Cited directly within written text	*Format:* Title of film or video (underlined or italicized). Writer/Director Name. Producer, Date of production. *Example:* English Composition. Thaiss, Chris & Nancy Shapiro. The Standard Deviants, 1997.
Internet source	(Norse)	Format: Author's last name, first name and middle name or initial. Description or "Title of article in quotation marks." Internet. (Date the article was posted, if given.) Available: <Internet address>. Date you accessed the material. *Example:* Norse, Ruth. "The Hijacking of American Education: Part I." Internet. Available: <http://www.forerunner.com/forerunner/X0282_Hijacking_American_L.html>. 4 Oct. 2001.

Example Citations (continued)

Type of Source	Sample In-Text Citation	Appearance on "Works Cited" Page
Anonymous Internet source	(Battlefield) *Note: Use first word or key word from title*	*Format:* Description or "Title of article in quotation marks." Internet. (Date the article was posted, if given.) Available: <Internet address>. Date you accessed the material. *Example:* "Battlefield: Vietnam." Internet. Available: <http://www.pbs.org/battfieldvietnam/timeline/index.html>. 21 Jan. 2005.
Reference CD-ROM with author	(Haskell)	*Format:* Author's Last Name, First Name. "Article title." *Publication Title* (underlined or italicized). Database (if any). CD-ROM. Database provider. Date of publication. *Example:* Haskell, Frank A. "The Battle of Gettysburg." *CD Sourcebook of American History.* CD-ROM. Folio Corporation. 1992-1994.
Reference CD-ROM with no author	Best cited directly within written text	*Format:* "Title of Article." *Encyclopedia Title* (underlined or italicized), year ed. CD-ROM. City of production: Producer, year of production. *Example:* "World War II." Webster's Concise Encyclopedia, 1996 ed. CD-ROM. Las Cruces: Sofsource, Inc. 1996.
E-mail	(Jones)	*Format:* Last name, first name of writer. "Title (if any)." E-mail to (name of recipient). Day Month and year of communication. *Examples:* Jones, Vanessa. "Recipe Instructions." E-mail to S. Barrett. 31 Aug. 2002. *or:* Jones, Vanessa. E-mail to the author. 31 Aug. 2002.
Personal interview	(Ellsworth)	*Format:* Last name, first name of person being interviewed. Personal interview. Day month and year of interview. *Example:* Ellsworth, William. Personal interview. 31 July 2002.
Telephone interview	(Needham)	*Format:* Last name, first name of person being interviewed. Telephone interview. Day month and year of interview. *Example:* Needham, Betty. Telephone interview. 7 Nov. 2002.
Published, recorded, or broadcast interviews	(Wiser)	*Format:* Last name, first name of person being interviewed. Interview with (interviewer). Publication or program (underlined). Day month and year of publication. *Example:* Wiser, Elizabeth. Interview with S. Barrett. Seniors Sound Off. 15 Sep. 2002.

APPENDIX E

Week 5 and Week 6
Paragraph Evaluation Form

Use to correct writing assignments on Weeks 5 and 6.

Name: _____

Assignment: _____ (11 points possible) Score: _____

Score	Item Evaluated (points possible)
_____	Topic Sentence (1)
_____	Content (2)
_____	Concluding sentence (1)
_____	Formality (no errors = 1; one error = .5; more errors = 0)
_____	Grammar (no errors = 1; one error = .5; more errors = 0)
_____	Spelling (no errors = 1; one error = .5; more errors = 0)
_____	Daily development of paragraph (1)
_____	Edited paragraph outline (1)
_____	Planning Outline (1)
_____	Brainstorming (1)

Comments:
_____
_____
_____
_____
_____
_____
_____
_____
_____

APPENDIX F

General Paragraph Evaluation Form

Use entire form to correct writing assignments on Weeks 9, 11, 14, 17, 20, 23, 26, 29, 32, and 35.

Name:_____

Assignment:_____

(100 points possible) Score:_____

Organization & Content: (7 pts each)

_____Topic sentence – states purpose, captures attention

_____Supporting points and details – topical and unified

_____Good use of facts and examples

_____Logical arrangement

_____Final sentence sums up paragraph

General Impression: (4 pts each)

_____Concise (avoids unnecessary words and phrases)

_____Includes necessary and complete explanation

_____Command of vocabulary

_____Uses strong verbs, descriptive adv. and adj.

_____Specific wording (not vague)

_____Flows well

_____Proper emphasis

_____Fulfills purpose, targets audience

_____Variety of sentence lengths and types

Mechanical Errors: spelling, grammar, formality

_____0 errors = +5 points; 1-2 = +2; 3 or more = 0

Other Requirements:

_____"Works Cited" page and in-text reference (4 pts).

_____Literary device (2 pts.)

_____Style points (3 pts.)

_____Checklist (10 pts.)

_____Outline, drafts, brainstorming (3 pts.)

_____Presentation (2 pts.)

Comments:

Paragraph Positives - _____

_____

_____

_____

_____

_____

_____

_____

_____

_____

Simple:_____ Complex:_____

Compound:_____ Cmpd-cmplx:_____

Improper:_____

_____

Improvement Ideas - _____

_____

_____

_____

_____

_____

_____

_____

_____

APPENDIX G

Week 10 Research & Documentation Evaluation Form

Name: _____   (94 points possible) **Total Score:** _____

		Points	Score	Comments:
Day 1				
8 Note cards		16	_____	_____
Working Bibliography		4	_____	_____
Day 2				
8 Note cards		16	_____	_____
Working Bibliography		4	_____	_____
Day 3				
8 Note cards		16	_____	_____
Working Bibliography		4	_____	_____
Day 4				
Quote #1	Proper quote	1	_____	_____
	Proper parenthetical reference	1	_____	_____
	Proper punctuation of reference	1	_____	_____
Quote #2	Proper quote	1	_____	_____
	Proper parenthetical reference	1	_____	_____
	Proper punctuation of reference	1	_____	_____
Quote #3	Proper quote	1	_____	_____
	Proper parenthetical reference	1	_____	_____
	Proper punctuation of reference	1	_____	_____
Works Cited Page				
	Proper title	1	_____	_____
	Source #1: Proper content & format	2	_____	_____
	Source #2: Proper content & format	2	_____	_____
	Source #3: Proper content & format	2	_____	_____
	Alphabetical order	1	_____	_____
Day 5				
Quote #1	Proper quote	1	_____	_____
	Proper parenthetical reference	1	_____	_____
	Proper punctuation of reference	1	_____	_____
Quote #2	Proper quote	1	_____	_____
	Proper parenthetical reference	1	_____	_____
	Proper punctuation of reference	1	_____	_____
Quote #3	Proper quote	1	_____	_____
	Proper parenthetical reference	1	_____	_____
	Proper punctuation of reference	1	_____	_____
Works Cited Page				
	Proper title	1	_____	_____
	Source #1: Proper content & format	2	_____	_____
	Source #2: Proper content & format	2	_____	_____
	Source #3: Proper content & format	2	_____	_____
	Alphabetical order	1	_____	_____

APPENDIX H

Timed Paragraph Evaluation Form

Use to correct in-class writing assignments on Weeks 15, 18, 21, 24, 27, 30, and 33.

Name:_____

Assignment:_____

(60 points possible) Score:_____

Organization & Content: (5 pts each)

_____Topic sentence

_____Logical arrangement

_____Content is on topic

_____Concluding sentence

_____Planning outline

Research & Documentation:

_____Research note cards (6 points)

_____Bibliographic information page (5 points)

_____In-text references (4 points)

_____"Works Cited" page (5 points)

Formality Errors:

_____0 errors = +4 points; 1-2 = +2; 3 or more = 0

Other Requirements:

_____Paragraph type fits assignment (4 points)

_____Proper length (4 points)

_____Proper format and order (3 points)

Comments:

Paragraph Positives - _____

_____

_____

_____

_____

_____

_____

_____

_____

_____

_____

Improvement Ideas - _____

_____

_____

_____

_____

_____

_____

_____

_____

_____

_____

APPENDIX I

Edit Evaluation Form
Use to correct editing on Weeks 13, 16, 19, 22, 25, 28, 31, and 34

Student Name: _____ Date: _____

Week # & Assignment _____ Class: _____

		Points Awarded (0 = no improvement)			
Check if applies	Categories to Improve	0	1	2	3
	Organization and content				
	General impression				
	Mechanical corrections				
	Other:				
	Other:				
	Other:				

Comments: _____

© 2002-2006 Steve and Shari Barrett. All rights reserved.

cut here - cut here

Edit Evaluation Form
Use to correct editing on Weeks 13, 16, 19, 22, 25, 28, 31, and 34

Student Name: _____ Date: _____

Week # & Assignment _____ Class: _____

		Points Awarded (0 = no improvement)			
Check if applies	Categories to Improve	0	1	2	3
	Organization and content				
	General impression				
	Mechanical corrections				
	Other:				
	Other:				
	Other:				

Comments: _____

APPENDIX J

Teaching Schedules

One Year Schedule	Two Year Schedule
Week 1 - Sentence Savvy Week 2 - Formal Writing Guidelines Week 3 - Purposes of Writing Week 4 - Writing Process Overview Week 5 - Paragraph Basics 1 Week 6 - Paragraph Basics 1 Week 7 - Paragraph Basics 2 Week 8 - Paragraph Basics 2 & Quiz Week 9 - Descriptive Paragraphs Week 10 - Research, Documentation, and Ownership of Ideas Week 11 - Definition Paragraph Week 12 - Thinking Like a Teacher Week 13 - Edit Descriptive Paragraph & Quiz Week 14 - Narrative Paragraph Week 15 - Timed Narrative Paragraph Week 16 - Edit Narrative Paragraph Week 17 - Process Paragraph Week 18 - Timed Process Paragraph Week 19 - Edit Process Paragraph & Quiz Week 20 - Comparison Paragraph Week 21 - Timed Comparison Paragraph Week 22 - Edit Comparison Paragraph Week 23 - Cause/Effect Paragraph Week 24 - Timed Cause/Effect Paragraph Week 25 - Edit Cause/Effect Paragraph & Quiz Week 26 - Analogy Paragraph Week 27 - Timed Analogy Paragraph Week 28 - Edit Analogy Paragraph Week 29 - Position Paragraph Week 30 - Timed Position Paragraph Week 31 - Edit Position Paragraph Week 32 - Character Analysis & Quiz Week 33 - Timed Character Analysis Week 34 - Edit Character Analysis Week 35 - Seeing the Big Picture Week 36 - Final Test	To teach this course over two years, allow two days per daily lesson. Thus, each weekly plan will be completed every two weeks. **Accelerated Schedule** Week 1 - Sentence Savvy & Formal Writing Guidelines Week 2 - Purposes of Writing & Writing Process Overview Week 3 - Paragraph Basics 1 (Week 5 & 6) Week 4 - Paragraph Basics 2 (Week 7 & 8) Week 5 - Descriptive Paragraphs & Research, Documentation, and Ownership of Ideas Week 6 - Definition Paragraph & Thinking Like a Teacher Week 7 - Narrative Paragraph & Edit Descriptive Paragraph Week 8 - Process Paragraph Week 9 - Timed Narrative Paragraph & Timed Process Paragraph Week 10 - Edit Narrative Paragraph & Process Paragraph Week 11 - Comparison Paragraph Week 12 - Cause/Effect Paragraph Week 13 - Timed Comparison Paragraph & Timed Cause/Effect Paragraph Week 14 - Edit Comparison Paragraph & Cause/Effect Paragraph Week 15 - Analogy Paragraph Week 16 - Position Paragraph Week 17 - Timed Analogy Paragraph & Timed Position Paragraph Week 18 - Edit Analogy Paragraph & Position Paragraph Week 19 - Character Analysis Week 20 - Seeing the Big Picture & Final Test

Selected Bibliography

Abrams, M. H. *A Glossary of Literary Terms*. New York: Rinehart & Company, 1958.

Barnet, Sylvan. *A Short Guide to Writing About Literature*. Fourth Edition. Boston: Little, Brown and Company, 1979.

Crews, Frederick., Sandra Schor, Michael Hennessy. *The Borzoi Handbook for Writers*. Third Edition. New York: McGraw-Hill, 1993.

Gibaldi, Joseph. *MLA Handbook for Writers of Research Papers*. Fourth Edition. New York: Modern Language Association of America, 1995.

Troyka, Lynn Quitman. *Simon & Schuster Handbook For Writers*. Fifth Edition. Upper Saddle River: Prentice Hall, 1999.

INDEX

Active voice, 12
Adjective, 52
Adjective clause, 53-54
Adverb, 52
Adverbial clause, 53
Adverbial phrase, 53
Alliteration, 126
Analogy, 151
Analogy paragraph, 151-153
Antecedent, 12
Auxiliary verb, 13, 199
Audience, 27

Bibliographic information, 72
Block quote, 73
Brainstorming, 28

Cause and effect paragraph, 137-139
Character analysis, 175-179
Cliché, 10
Colloquial wording, 9
Comparison paragraph, 123-126
Complex sentence, 2-3
Compound sentences, 1-2
Compound-complex sentences, 3
Concluding sentence, 39, 87
Conjunctive adverbs, 2, 199
Contention, 19
Contraction, 9
Coordinate ideas, 38, 40
Coordinating conjunction, 1

Definition paragraph, 81-83
Dependent clause, 2
Descriptive paragraph, 63-65

Emphatic location, 4
Essay components, 187-188
Evaluation forms, 206-210

Formal writing, 9
Formality rules, 9, 200

Grading (Evaluation) forms, 206-210
Grammar rules, 11-13, 200

Helping verb, 13, 199
Hyperbole, 113

Independent clause, 1
Infinitive, 53
Infinitive phrase, 53
Informal writing, 9
Integrated quotes, 73
Interjection, 11

Literary device, 54
Logical proof, 164-165
Logical sequence, 64-65

Metaphor, 100
MLA documentation, 74-76, 202-205
Narrative paragraph, 97-100
Nominalization, 11
Note cards, 72
Noun, 51
Number, 12

Overstatement, 113

Page format, 70
Paragraph checklist, 201
Parallelism, 82
Paraphrase, 73-74
Parenthetical reference (citation), 75-76
Participial phrase, 53
Participle, 52
Passive voice, 13
Person, 10, 12, 112
Personification, 140
Phrase, 52
Plagiarism, 71-72
Planning outline, 29-31, 40
Post hoc, ergo, propter hoc, 139
Preposition, 53, 200
Preposition, ending with, 11
Prepositional phrase, 53
Process paragraph, 111-113

Quotation, 73

INDEX - continued

Research, 71-74
Rhetorical question, 166
Rough draft, 31

Sentence fragment, 11
Simile, 66
Simple sentence, 1
Slang, 10
State of being verb, 5, 51, 199
Style points, 52-54, 200
Subject - verb agreement, 12
Subordinate clause, 2
Subordinate ideas, 38-40
Subordinating conjunction, 2-3, 199
Supporting details, 29-31
Supporting information, 29-31, 38, 87
Summary, 73-74

Teaching schedule, 211
Tense, 12
Topic sentence, 28, 31, 37-38, 87
Transition sentences, 39
Transitions words, 38-39

Under-supported contention, 165
Unsupported contention, 20
Understatement, 113
Use of an idea, 113

Verb, 51
Verb tense, 12

Working Bibliography, 72
Works Cited page, 76
Works consulted, 76